More RETRO DINER

A Second Helping of Roadside Recipes

RANDY GARBIN AND TERI DUNN

COLLECTORS PRESS

PORTLAND, OREGON

Designers: Kevin A. Welsch and Matthew H. Fitchen, Collectors Press, Inc.
Editor: Sue Mann
Proofreader: Jade Chan

Library of Congress Cataloging-in-Publication Data

Garbin, Randy.
  More retro diner : a second helping of roadside recipes / by Randy Garbin
& Teri Dunn.-- 1st American ed.
      p.   cm.   -- (Retro series)
  Includes index.
  ISBN 1-933112-09-3 (hardcover : alk. paper)
  1. Cookery, American. 2. Diners (Restaurants)--United States. I. Dunn,
Teri. II. Title. III. Series.
  TX715.G197 2005
  641.5973--dc22

                              2005013203

Printed in Singapore
9 8 7 6 5 4 3 2 1

Collectors Press books are available at special discounts for bulk purchases, premiums, and promotions. Special editions, including personalized inserts or covers, and corporate logos, can be printed in quantity for special purposes. For further information contact: Special Sales, Collectors Press, Inc., P.O. Box 230986, Portland, OR 97281.
Toll free: 1-800-423-1848.

For a free catalog write to: Collectors Press, Inc., P.O. Box 230986, Portland, OR 97281.
Toll free: 1-800-423-1848 or collectorspress.com.

Your **free enhanced version** of this book is at www.enhancedbooks.com! Visit today.

193☐311☐20☐93

To Cecelia, with whom I look forward to sharing the road as soon as she gets out of diapers. —Randy Garbin

With thanks to Jill Rodgers, wherever she may be! And to Ted Putnam, the best comfort-food cook I know. —Teri Dunn

Contents

Introduction

Americans are enjoying a renewed love affair with the American diner and the trend toward serving home-cooked meals by real people in real places. Despite this renewal, stories continue to appear in everything from the *New York Times* to the *East Podunk Bugle* heralding, in some fashion, the decline and disappearance of the Great American Diner. However, as followers of this renewal and of the industry for fifteen years, we see the diner continuing to satisfy a growing share of the American public. Granted, we will probably never again see the landscape quite as populated with those gleaming ladies of the roadside, but someone somewhere will always restore a tired old vintage diner or build a new version, updated for the demands of modern society.

The story of the diner's origins have finally seeped into the cultural consciousness; we can safely say that at any given moment, you will likely find someone in your local diner who can tell you about Walter Scott of Providence, Rhode Island, and how he began with his diminutive, horse-drawn carriage converted into a no-frills lunch wagon seven years after the end of the Civil War. Some may overstate Scott's role somewhat: the idea of food on wheels hardly started with him. We do know with some certainty, however, that the lineage of what became a thriving industry of constructing high-quality, stylish, turnkey restaurants traces to this humble start. We've estimated that the diner has served more than 22 billion meals in the 133 years since Scott first started offering "chewed" sandwiches, pie, and hot coffee to his late-night customers.

The story of the diner business largely follows the same progress and decline of most industries born in the Industrial Revolution. The innovations that came after Scott's produced one of the most distinct hallmarks of American ingenuity, quality and style. In a sense those qualities made rediscovery of the diner's architectural form inevitable.

The diner is universally acknowledged as the quintessential American restaurant. When Americans see a diner, they instinctively recognize it as a place to eat. Though some may still regard the old diner as a greasy-spoon truck stop, more likely people will see it as a bastion of good comfort food served in a solidly constructed building that someone fashioned in a factory, probably in New Jersey. The diner

world now has books describing everything from its history to the culture it fosters to the food it serves. It starred in a movie, thanks to Barry Levenson. It has a magazine, several Web sites, and an ongoing historical exhibit at the Johnson & Wales University Culinary Archives in Providence.

We see no end to the diner's influence on design and cuisine. This trend looks even more remarkable in light of its informal and largely blue-collar origins. Schools of architecture did not hold classes in diner design. Innovations in the industry generally came from dozens of unsung heroes who worked at drafting tables applying design ideas derived from industry colleagues and other outside influences. Though today we can identify a few individuals responsible for some of the more iconic aspects of the diner, most changes came

. . . how about a milkshake?

through seat-of-the-pants inspiration, evolution, and outright copying.

Diners' menus usually took their cues from their communities. Diners in French-Canadian neighborhoods likely served meat pie. In Italian enclaves eggs came with Italian sausage. In Jewish neighborhoods matzo ball soup was on the menu. Family recipes were refined through generations, then scaled up for commercial food service.

Highway diners tended to standardize around the basics, putting a greater emphasis on consistency and service. Popular with truckers, these operations benefited from word of mouth that could spread throughout the entire region and beyond. However, most diners-as-truck-stops ended with the development of the interstate highway system; though the myth persists, the idea that one can judge a restaurant by the number of trucks parked outside

ended in the late 1950s with the
Eisenhower administration. Truckers
today concern themselves more with
parking and portions than with the
subtleties of how the cook seasons
the soup.

The insatiable American desire for
constant innovation had the regret-
table side effect of casting aside and
destroying much of the diners'
beautiful flamboyance. The diner-
building industry finally shed many
of its practitioners and what we call
the "transportation metaphor" in the

1960s. (Since Scott's days diners either
had moved or had looked like they
moved, looking like space ports as the
era ended.) Despite the race to put a
man on the moon, America's domestic
styling preferences turned inward and
sought more familiar comforts. With
design cues coming from colonial and
early-American influences, boomerangs
and starbursts succumbed to wagon
wheels and Chippendale styles.

Diners became victims of the change as
well, and the romance began to cool. In
what seemed to be the final step in its

evolution, the busy neighborhood diner
became just another family restaurant,
laden with all the burdens the concept
imposed. Though the counter remained,
the grill disappeared deep into the
kitchen. The banter between the grill
man and the customers ended. The
personal touch offered by waitress
service remained, but the larger
operations of these restaurants did not
allow for the same kind of impromptu
theater more commonly found in
the smaller neighborhood diners.
Menus expanded as well, usually to
several pages. Suddenly, the new diners

seemed to specialize in *every dish ever made*, from a grilled cheese sandwich to rigatoni à la vodka. In many places you could still get pancakes at four in the afternoon, but your friend could get chicken Florentine.

Today, Americans appreciate the diner for many reasons, not the least of which is the food. They go to restaurants primarily to eat, but go to the diner for something more than just nutrition. Those lucky enough to live near neighborhood diners can tell stories of

the people they've met there as much as they talk about the meals they've eaten. Over coffee their experiences sweeten with wry comments from world-weary waitresses, from the joy of watching grill men effortlessly orchestrate the preparation of a dozen meals simultaneously, from hearty handshakes and smiles received when they meet the owner. On those occasions, which come with increasing rarity in the modern world, they feel restored. All seems right with the world.

That said, our favorite diners are still the ones that serve the most amazing meals—not Wolfgang Puck-amazing, but amazing because every bite of that meatloaf completely satisfies a craving that started a couple of hours earlier. Amazing because we may have had that meatloaf a hundred times before, but every time we order it, we sigh gratefully relieved that our memory didn't embelish the last experience. This is how it always tastes and how it always *will* taste. Contending with so many changes, we find catharsis in the consistency of that meatloaf.

People often pigeonhole diner cuisine into a rather simple formula of meat and mashed potatoes; eggs, bacon, and pancakes; hot coffee; Cokes and club sandwiches. However, the best diners break with traditions and will experiment. They will serve up the better examples of regional specialties and adjust to the changes in public taste. Some of our favorites now serve tasty Tex-Mex along with fresh vegetarian selections; some take on old classics and give them new spins. The diner owner who tells us, "We serve your typical diner food, but we use fresh ingredients," makes us fans for life.

This book, then, is another bit of proof that the diner remains and will continue to remain an important part of American heritage. Some recipes we've included come from operating diners and the generosity of their owners.

Keep in mind that we've made every effort to properly reduce the quantities of some recipes, which called for serving dozens, to a more manageable quantity.

The diner industry continues to evolve, with new people and new recipes keeping it fresh and vibrant. As long as you continue to value quality meals and the personal touch, there will always be a seat waiting for you at your local diner.

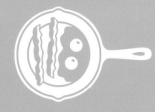

Up & at 'Em!

In most parts of America, the word *diner* means breakfast. Any diner that can't serve up a decent breakfast should just turn off the lights, lock the doors, and call it a day. To some, a diner that doesn't serve breakfast all day hardly qualifies as a true diner. However, we don't agree; this rule would exclude dozens of smaller diners that must clear space on their grills for the more savory lunch and dinner items.

These days breakfast remains diners' most popular meal. In New England, where most diners serve only breakfast and lunch, a good diner often generates the bulk of its revenues from weekend breakfasts. People skip the hearty breakfast on weekdays, but on weekends they look forward to a big plate of pancakes or french toast or a three-egg omelet hot off the grill.

With some subtle tinkering, breakfast can really shine. Sweet potato pancakes will win out over the plain variety, and any diner that makes its own corned beef hash rises on our favorites list. Knowing that such hard-to-reach places as the Deluxe Town Diner in Watertown, Massachusetts, or the Miss Albany Diner in Albany, New York, serve their own recipes for hash motivates us to take many lengthy road-trip pilgrimages.

We also find solace in the simple things: fresh hot coffee made with a strong but not a bitter blend, yellow-as-sunshine omelets without a hint of browning, and pancakes light and fluffy served with real maple syrup. Please note: The fake stuff will not do; we often bring our own supply of real syrup. (We've never had difficulty; we're saving the owner a little money. If real maple syrup is on the menu, however, we order it no matter the

cost.) Unfortunately, most places serve corn syrup varieties. The one regional exception is Vermont, where no self-respecting breakfast joint would serve the fake stuff.

We also enjoy some of the more outlandish practices at little diners struggling for attention: diners with mega-sized "everything" omelets like the Capitol Diner in Lynn, Massachusetts, or the spicy breakfast

burritos served at the Blue Benn in Bennington, Vermont. No diner outdoes the portions at Carl's Oxford Diner in Oxford, Massachusetts. Order yourself a couple of eggs, bacon, and fries, and stand back as Paul the grill man presents you with *three* eggs, *six* slices of bacon, and a *separate plate for a small mountain* of home fries. If you have the capacity to finish this feast and the audacity to ask for more, you'll get it.

Miss Adams's Breakfast Casserole

1. Preheat the oven to 350 degrees.

2. Melt 3/4 stick butter in large skillet and sauté peppers and onions until soft. Add garlic, oregano, pepper, and cayenne; stir.

3. Butter a 4-inch-deep pan and line with 1-inch bread cubes. Sprinkle 2 cups cheese over bread. Sprinkle ham over cheese. Add vegetable layer and remaining 2 cups cheese. Sprinkle on thin layer of very small bread cubes.

4. Whisk eggs and half-and-half together in large bowl. Pour over bread cubes as evenly as possible.

5. Cover pan with foil.

6. Bake 1 hour. Uncover and cook a little longer until casserole is set in the center. It should shake uniformly.

Serves 6

3/4 stick (12 tbsps) unsalted
    butter, plus additional for
    baking pan
6 cups sweet peppers, diced
3 cups Bermuda onions, diced
2 cloves garlic, pressed
3/4 tbsp dried oregano
1/2 tsp black pepper
pinch cayenne
9 cups bread ends cut into
    1-inch cubes
4 cups grated cheddar
    cheese, divided
12 oz. ham, diced
1 slice bread ends, cubed
    very small
8 eggs
4 1/2 cups half-and-half

Jigger's Pumpkin Pancakes

1. Mix together flour, baking powder, sugar, salt, and spices.

2. Stir in milk, pumpkin, eggs, vanilla extract, and bacon drippings.

3. Preheat and grease griddle or skillet with butter. Use about 1 cup of batter per pancake and cook, flipping only once. Serve warm with real maple syrup.

Serves 4

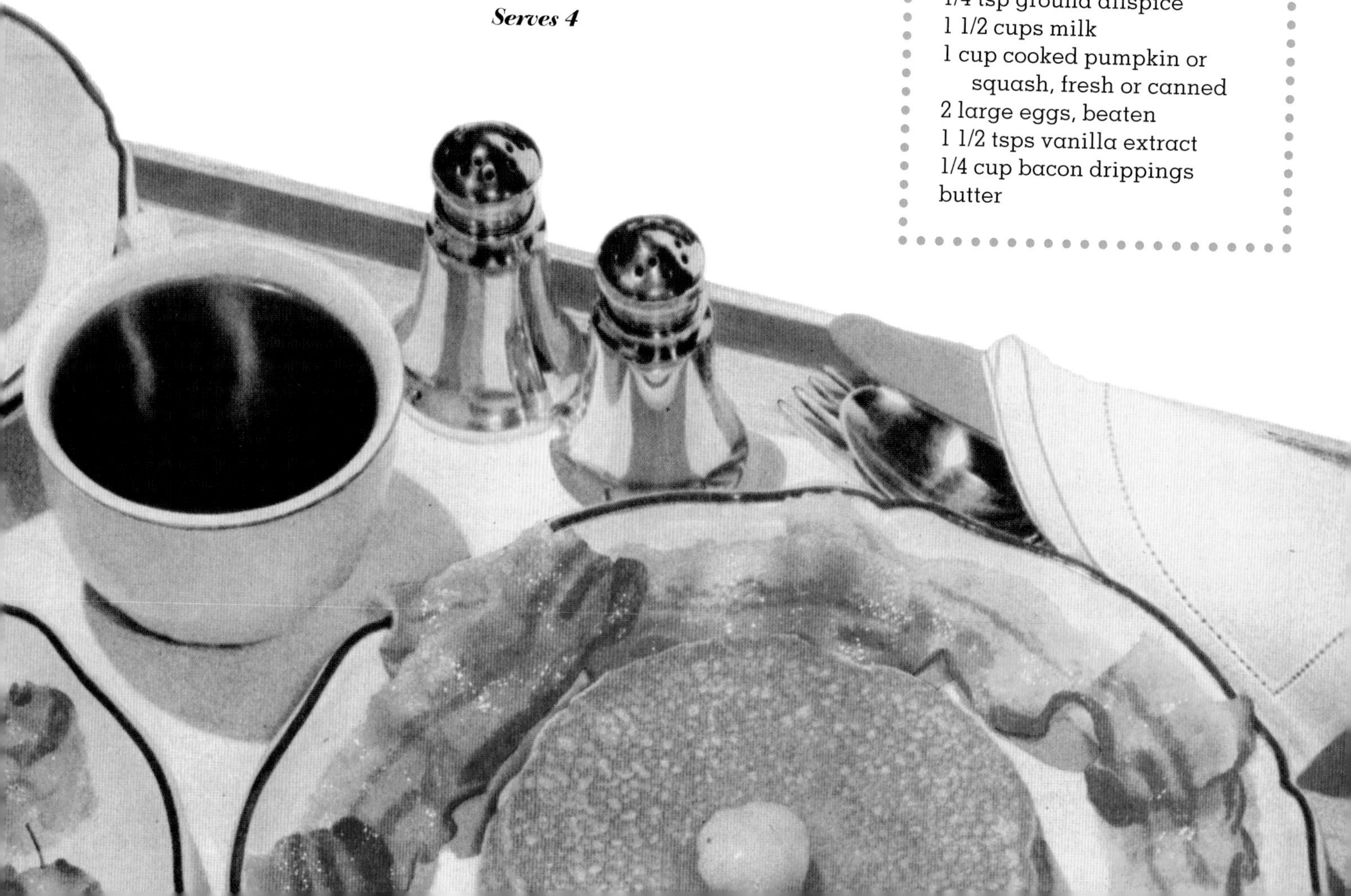

1 3/4 cups white flour
2 tsps baking powder
4 tbsps light brown sugar
1 tsp salt
1 tsp ground cinnamon
1/4 tsp ground cloves
1 tsp ground ginger
1/4 tsp ground allspice
1 1/2 cups milk
1 cup cooked pumpkin or
    squash, fresh or canned
2 large eggs, beaten
1 1/2 tsps vanilla extract
1/4 cup bacon drippings
butter

Miss Adams's Master Muffins

This recipe is a base; you think up your own additions. At the Miss Adams Diner, they make rhubarb-oat bran, pineapple-corn, poppyseed-sour cream, butterscotch-pecan, date-pecan, peanut butter-chocolate chip, sunflower-raisin bran, plum-yogurt, raspberry-corn, and more. Just plain blueberry is probably the most popular.

1. Preheat oven to 350 degrees.

2. Mix oil, honey, and egg together.

3. Mix buttermilk, baking soda, salt, and vanilla extract in separate bowl.

4. Whisk flours and wheat germ together in another bowl to blend.

5. Combine all mixtures until barely incorporated. Fold in choice of fruit or nuts or both.

6. Spoon into muffin cups. Push batter down and mound above level of cup.

7. Bake about 20 minutes, rotate baking tins for even baking, and bake 5–10 minutes more.

8. Cool briefly and remove from tins.

Makes 12 muffins

2/3 cup corn oil
3/4 cup honey
1 egg, beaten
1 cup buttermilk
1 tsp baking soda
1 tsp salt
1 tsp vanilla extract
2 cups white flour
1 1/2 cups whole-wheat
  pastry flour
1/2 cup wheat germ or bran
1 1/2 cups fruit (apple, pears,
  blueberries, peaches, or
  your choice), diced
3/4 cup toasted nuts
  (walnuts, pecans,
  almonds, or your
  choice), chopped

Popovers

1. Preheat oven to 400 degrees.

2. Mix flour, salt, and sugar in large bowl.

3. Mix butter, milk, and eggs in small bowl. Add to large bowl and beat thoroughly until smooth, or use a blender.

4. Grease muffin tin or genuine cast iron popover pan. Pour in 1/2 cup batter per popover.

5. Bake 40 minutes. Do not open oven; a blast of cold air will cause popovers to collapse. Check during final 5 minutes so tops don't get too browned. Popovers should be dark golden brown with a moist interior.

6. Serve hot.

Serves 8–12

- 1 cup bread flour, presifted
- 1/4 tsp salt
- 1 1/2 tbsps sugar
- 1 tbsp butter, melted
- 1 cup milk, at room temperature
- 2 eggs

Woody's Sweet Potato Muffins

1. Preheat oven to 350 degrees.

2. Cream butter and sugar in large bowl. Add eggs one at a time, beating after each addition. Add 1/3 of the flour; mix lightly. Stir in sweet potato. Add 1/3 of the flour; mix lightly.

3. Add coffee, walnuts, salt, spices, baking soda, and remaining 1/3 flour. Mix until blended. Do not overmix or muffins will be tough.

4. Fill muffin tins 3/4 full.

5. Bake 25 minutes or until inserted toothpick comes out clean.

Makes 12 muffins

- 3/4 pound (3 sticks) butter, softened
- 4 cups sugar
- 6 eggs
- 4 3/4 cups flour, divided
- 3 cups canned puréed sweet potatoes, drained and mashed
- 1 cup strong coffee
- 1 1/2 cups walnuts, chopped
- 1 1/2 tsps salt
- 1 1/2 tsps ground cinnamon
- 2 1/4 tsps ground nutmeg
- 1/4 tsp ground allspice
- 3 tsps baking soda

Whole-wheat Waffles

1. Preheat waffle iron.

2. Combine cider vinegar and milk; let stand a few minutes until mixture begins to curdle.

3. Mix flours, wheat germ, sugar, baking powder, and salt in large bowl.

4. Beat eggs in separate large bowl. Add milk mixture and mix thoroughly. Pour in melted butter; stir.

5. Pour dry ingredients into wet ingredients and stir with wooden spoon only until just mixed. Do not overbeat.

6. Scoop 1 cup or less batter, depending on waffle iron's size, onto waffle iron and cook. Check after 1–2 minutes so waffle doesn't overcook. Serve hot with butter and real maple syrup.

Makes 6–8 waffles

1 tsp cider vinegar
1 cup milk
1 cup white flour
1 cup whole-wheat flour
1/3 cup wheat germ
1/3 cup sugar
2 1/2 tsps baking powder
1/2 tsp salt
3 eggs
1/2 stick (4 tbsps) butter, melted

Judi's Sour Cream Coffee Cake

1. Preheat oven to 350 degrees. Butter and flour tube or bundt pan.

2. Mix butter, sugar, eggs, sour cream, and vanilla extract in large bowl until well blended.

3. Mix flour, baking powder, baking soda, and salt thoroughly in separate large bowl.

4. Mix wet ingredients into dry, stirring well.

5. Press 1/3 batter into pan. Sprinkle 1/2 filling over batter. Press 1/3 batter over filling.

6. Reserve a few teaspoons filling for topping; set aside. Sprinkle remaining filling over batter. Spoon remainder of batter over filling; lightly sprinkle top with reserved filling.

7. Bake 1 hour or until toothpick inserted comes out clean.

8. Let cool 15–20 minutes before removing from pan and serving.

To make filling:

Mix all ingredients in small bowl and set aside.

Serves 6–8

---

2 sticks butter, at room
   temperature
1 1/2 cups sugar
3 eggs
1 1/2 cups sour cream
1 1/2 tsps vanilla extract
3 cups white flour
1 1/2 tsps baking powder
1 1/2 tsps baking soda
1/4 tsp salt
filling (see recipe below),
   divided

Filling:
3/4 cup brown sugar
3/4 cup walnuts
2 tsps ground cinnamon

Frank's Veggie Omelet

1. Gently beat eggs and herbs in bowl with just a splash of water.

2. Heat heavy metal pan and melt butter. Add shallots. They will sizzle as they simmer.

3. Add eggs when shallots start making cracking sounds and look a little mushy. Swirl eggs around; reduce heat.

4. Lift pan and tap firmly on burner. This "settles" eggs and evens out the final appearance. Every so often redistribute eggs by gently swirling and tapping pan, tilting it so uncooked eggs are cooked equally.

5. Add cheese when egg layer is cooked.

6. Add vegetables last, cooking only 1 or 2 minutes or until more steam comes from pan. A finished omelet should have no brown spots.

7. Hold serving plate in one hand and pan in the other. Slide edge of omelet out of pan. Fold rest of omelet over edge in thirds onto plate.

8. Garnish with sour cream and green onions. Serve with toast and sliced fruit, if desired.

Serves 1

3 medium to large eggs per person
1/2 tsp *fines herbes* (commercially available herb mixture of chervil, parsley, thyme, and tarragon)
1 tsp unsalted butter
3 tbsps minced shallot
1/3 cup grated sharp cheddar cheese
fresh vegetables of choice (orange bell peppers, mushrooms, spinach, etc.), sliced
dollop sour cream
4 tbsps green onions

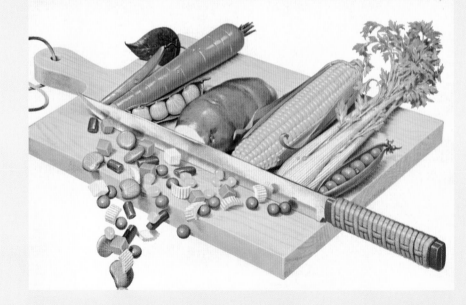

Asparagus & Cheese Quiche

1. Sauté onion in oil; let cool slightly.

2. Pour milk into saucepan and scald (heat until steaming, but not boiling). Let cool slightly.

3. Preheat oven to 375 degrees.

4. Scatter asparagus in bottom of pie shell.

5. Retrieve onion with slotted spoon to avoid taking too much oil; scatter in pie shell. Evenly distribute cheese over asparagus and onion.

6. Beat eggs in large bowl; add nutmeg, salt, and pepper. Trickle hot milk in, stirring constantly. Pour custard mixture carefully into pie shell.

7. Set pie shell on baking sheet; bake 30–35 minutes or until top is golden brown and custard is "set."

Serves 4

1 medium onion, diced
1 tsp vegetable oil
2 cups milk
6 asparagus spears, diced
1 9-inch unbaked single
    crust pie shell
1 cup grated cheddar cheese
3 eggs
pinch ground nutmeg
salt and black pepper,
    to taste

Eggs in Purgatory

1 large onion, diced
1 tsp crushed Italian red
    pepper flakes
2 tbsps olive oil
2 28-oz. cans crushed
    tomatoes
1 8-oz. can tomato paste
1 1/2 cups water, dry white
    wine, or mixture of both
2 tbsps dried basil
1 1/2 tbsps dried oregano
salt and white pepper, to
    taste
1 tbsp white vinegar
2 eggs

1. Sauté onion and red pepper in oil in large skillet. Add tomatoes and tomato paste and stir. Add water and mix well. Add basil, oregano, salt, and pepper.

2. Simmer mixture 10–15 minutes until it reduces somewhat. (If it becomes too thick, add water.)

3. Poach eggs in water and vinegar in separate pan until nearly cooked (yolk almost firm).

4. Using a slotted spoon, move eggs to pan with tomato mixture to finish poaching.

5. Carefully divide onto two plates and serve hot.

Serves 2

New Orleans-style French Toast

1. Combine eggs, milk, vanilla extract, and cinnamon in large bowl; set batter aside.

2. Melt 1 tbsp butter in pan and sauté bananas and pecans until soft but not mushy.

3. Melt 4 tbsps butter in a large skillet over low heat.

4. Soak bread slices in batter.

5. Raise heat under melted butter and fry soaked bread until golden-brown on both sides, turning once.

6. Ladle 1–2 spoonfuls of banana-pecan mixture over each slice.

7. Pour several ounces of sauce over everything and serve at once.

To make sauce:

1. Melt butter in large skillet; stir in brown sugar. Remove from heat when well blended.

2. Add vanilla extract and brandy, if using; mix well. Sauce should be rather thick.

Serves 4–6

- 4 eggs
- 2 cups milk
- 1 tsp vanilla extract
- 1 tsp ground cinnamon
- 5 tbsps butter, divided
- 2 to 3 ripe bananas, sliced
- 3/4 cup pecans, crushed
- 1 loaf challah or french bread, cut into 1-inch slices
- sauce (see recipe right)

Sauce:
- 1 stick unsalted butter
- 1 cup dark brown sugar
- 1 tsp vanilla extract
- 1/4 cup brandy (optional)

Monterey Café Breakfast Burrito

1. Lay each tortilla on plate and spread with thin layer of salsa.

2. Sprinkle cheese and cilantro over salsa.

3. Beat eggs well in bowl, adding milk, salt, and pepper.

4. Scramble eggs in saucepan over medium heat, adding onion and tomato as eggs cook.

5. Spoon egg mixture in wide strip down middle of each tortilla.

6. Roll tortillas loosely into burrito style on plate, seam side down.

7. Place completed burritos and plates in hot oven a few minutes or briefly under broiler to reheat everything and melt cheese.

8. Serve piping hot with extra salsa and a dollop of sour cream on the side.

Serves 2

2 large fresh flour tortillas
hot salsa, divided
1/2 cup grated Monterey
    Jack cheese
handful fresh
    cilantro, chopped
4 eggs
dash milk
salt and black pepper,
    to taste
1 small onion, diced
1 tomato, diced
sour cream, for garnish

Banana-Bran Muffins

1. Preheat oven to 375 degrees. Grease muffin tin.

2. Mash bananas in large bowl; add brown sugar and mix thoroughly. Add egg, vanilla, cinnamon, and oil; mix.

3. Add dry ingredients and mix just to moisten.

4. Spoon batter into muffin cups.

5. Bake 15–20 minutes or until golden brown on top and a toothpick inserted comes out clean.

6. Serve slightly cooled with butter. Good with apricot jam or honey!

Serves 12

3 ripe bananas, mashed
1/2 cup brown sugar
1 egg
1 tsp vanilla extract
1 tsp ground cinnamon
1/3 cup vegetable oil
3/4 cup white flour
3/4 cup wheat flour
1/2 cup oat bran
2 tsps baking powder
1/2 tsp baking soda
1/4 tsp salt

Cheese-Custard Flan

1. Preheat oven to 325 degrees. Butter 9-inch glass pie plate or 9 x 4-inch loaf pan.

2. Scald milk in large saucepan over medium heat until steaming but not boiling. Lower heat and stir in cheese until all is melted.

3. Remove pan from stove and mix in onion, cayenne, salt, and pepper. Beat in eggs, one at a time, blending well after each addition.

4. Pour flan mixture into pan; cover loosely with foil.

5. Place pan in larger glass pan. Pour enough water in larger pan to measure 1/2 inch up side of flan pan.

6. Bake 30–40 minutes, checking frequently near the end. Water in the larger pan will bubble and may need to be replenished; add carefully so water doesn't splash onto flan. Flan is done when top is golden brown and knife inserted comes out clean.

7. Cool slightly before serving.

Serves 4

- 1 3/4 cups milk
- 1 cup grated mild cheddar or Monterey Jack cheese
- 1/4 cup onion, grated small
- 1/4 tsp cayenne
- salt and black pepper, to taste
- 3 eggs

Barney's Johnnycake

1. Combine vinegar and milk in large bowl; let stand a few minutes.

2. Preheat oven to 350 degrees. Grease two 9-inch pie plates.

3. Mix brown sugar, eggs, and shortening in another bowl until smooth. Add cornmeal, flour, salt, and baking soda; blend well. Stir in vinegar-milk mixture; mix until smooth.

4. Bake 45 minutes or until top is cracked and cakes have pulled away from sides of pans.

5. Cool and serve. A popular way to serve johnnycake is to break it into bite-size chunks in a bowl, sprinkle brown sugar over it, pour on milk, and eat it like cereal.

Serves 4–6

3 tbsps cider vinegar
3 cups milk
3/4 cup brown sugar
2 large eggs
3/4 cup shortening
3 1/4 cups cornmeal
1 1/2 cups white flour
1 1/2 tsps salt
2 1/2 tsps baking soda

Inviting Soups & Stews

Never underestimate the power of soup. Its fabled ability to cure colds, its seductive lure on a cold winter day, and its general ubiquity speak to the honored place it holds on American tables. Just the thought of hot soup, thick with ingredients and made from homemade stock, warms us all. The memory (real or imagined) of sitting in a small-town diner on a snowy day with a bowl of hot tomato served with a grilled cheese sandwich evokes a Rockwellian scene. Soup's power is evident in a story we heard of a customer who broke into his favorite diner late one night and filched a pint of its famous cream of mushroom soup.

For some a great soup is a meal in itself. Diners famous for their soups include O'Rourke's in Middletown, Connecticut, where owner Brian O'Rourke arrives every morning at 2:00 for his 4:00 opening. First he prepares the soup for his busy lunch trade, then bakes the breads that accompany his much-loved concoctions. For great chowder, few can beat the award-winning effort served at the Maine Diner in Wells, Maine. Brothers Myles and Dick Henry have owned this burgeoning Maine institution long enough to see three million customers pass through, with no signs of letup. The brothers credit their chowder (as well as many lobster dishes) as one of the biggest reasons for the diner's popularity.

Soup provides all of us with opportunities to prove our abilities and display our creativity. Its preparation allows a broad range of tinkering and gives chefs considerable leeway. We therefore encourage you to experiment with these recipes, especially after you've become comfortable with them and with your abilities. Though we have no supporting evidence, we suspect that the most amazing meals often happen entirely by accident. Here's to more happy accidents.

Shawn's Beef & Apple Stew

- 2 pounds beef chuck, trimmed and cut into 1-inch pieces
- 1/4 cup brown sugar
- 1/2 tsp ground nutmeg
- salt and black pepper, to taste
- 2 tbsps oil
- 2 cups dark beer, divided
- 1 tbsp butter
- 1/2 cup onion, diced
- 4 cloves garlic, diced
- 2 tbsps white flour
- 2 tbsps tomato paste
- 2 cups chicken stock
- 1 cinnamon stick
- 1 tbsp mustard
- 2 medium apples, peeled, cored, and chopped into 1-inch pieces

1. Sprinkle beef with brown sugar and nutmeg; toss in large bowl. Add salt and pepper.

2. Heat oil in large skillet over high heat until almost smoking. Brown beef pieces, working quickly. Turn off heat and return beef to bowl.

3. Pour 1 1/2 cups beer into skillet; let bubble. Scrape bottom and sides of pan. Set pan aside.

4. Melt butter on low heat in large, heavy stewpot; cook onion until soft, about 5 minutes. Add garlic and cook 1 minute. Add flour, increase heat, and cook about 2 minutes stirring constantly. Lower heat; add tomato paste and beer from skillet as well as any juices that have accumulated in bowl with meat. Stir in stock and add cinnamon stick. Stir in meat.

5. Bring to a boil, lower heat, and simmer 1 1/2 hours. Liquid will thicken and beef will become tender.

6. Stir in mustard and apple pieces 5 minutes before serving. Continue to simmer.

7. Stir in remaining 1/2 cup beer immediately before serving. Serve hot over mashed potatoes.

Serves 4–6

Black Bean & Macaroni Soup

1. Sauté onions in oil in large skillet over medium heat a few minutes until soft. Add garlic and cook 1 minute. Sprinkle oregano into skillet and stir well. Cook another minute or so. Turn off heat and set skillet aside.

2. Heat stock, tomatoes, and beans in large soup or stew pot. Scrape in onion-garlic mixture. Add wine, sugar, bay leaf, salt, and pepper. Simmer over low heat 1 hour, stirring occasionally. Soup will reduce slightly.

3. Add macaroni and cook 30 minutes.

4. Add bell pepper and corn 5 minutes before serving; stir well. Add water if soup seems too thick.

5. Serve piping hot, garnished with a sprinkling of fresh parsley, a grating of Parmesan cheese, or both.

Serves 4–6

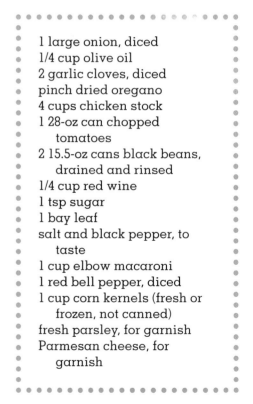

1 large onion, diced
1/4 cup olive oil
2 garlic cloves, diced
pinch dried oregano
4 cups chicken stock
1 28-oz can chopped
    tomatoes
2 15.5-oz cans black beans,
    drained and rinsed
1/4 cup red wine
1 tsp sugar
1 bay leaf
salt and black pepper, to
    taste
1 cup elbow macaroni
1 red bell pepper, diced
1 cup corn kernels (fresh or
    frozen, not canned)
fresh parsley, for garnish
Parmesan cheese, for
    garnish

Shawmut Diner Caciola

This stew claims its roots from the Caribbean, France, Portugal, and Spain.

1. Combine all ingredients except oil in large bowl. Cover and refrigerate overnight.

2. Remove meat from marinade using slotted spoon; reserve marinade.

3. Heat oil in Dutch oven or large, heavy pot over high heat. Brown meat on all sides, in batches if necessary. Stir in marinade, reduce the heat to low, cover, and simmer 1 hour or until meat is tender.

Serves 12

5 pounds boneless pork, cut into 1-inch pieces
5 cups dry red wine
5 cups dry white wine
1/2 cup sweet Hungarian paprika
1 tsp ground cinnamon
1 tsp red pepper flakes
1/4 cup garlic, minced
salt, to taste
1 tbsp onion, diced
1/4 cup vegetable oil or bacon fat

HOME OF THE SOUVENIR WINE JUG

Chicken-Corn Chowder

1. Heat stock, water, and potatoes in heavy stew pot. Lower heat to simmer and add chicken. Partially cover pot and cook about 20 minutes. Remove cooked chicken with slotted spoon and set aside. When cool, cut chicken into bite-size pieces, discarding skin and bones. Set aside.

2. Cook bacon in heavy skillet until browned on both sides but not crispy. Remove with slotted spoon and drain on paper towels. Set aside.

3. Sauté onion and celery in bacon grease. When onion is soft, remove onion and celery with slotted spoon and drain on paper towels. Set aside.

4. Add half-and-half, corn, thyme, and pepper to stock and potatoes. Stir in bacon and celery. Simmer, uncovered, about 5 minutes.

5. Add chicken pieces to pot. Simmer 5 minutes or so, stirring constantly. Serve hot.

Serves 4–6

3 cups chicken stock
2 cups water
4 potatoes, peeled and diced
1 1/2 pounds chicken breast meat
3 cups half-and-half
3 cups corn kernels (fresh or frozen, not canned)
4 slices hickory-smoked bacon
1 onion, diced
3 ribs celery, diced
1 tsp dried thyme
black pepper, to taste

Louise's Chicken-Tortilla Soup

This is the Southwestern version of cures-whatever-ails-you chicken soup.

1. Heat oil in Dutch oven over medium heat.

2. Add onion and garlic; sauté 2 minutes. Stir in chicken.

3. Add corn, wine, chiles, cumin, Worcestershire sauce, chili powder, broth, tomatoes, and tomato soup. Stir well. Bring to a boil, reduce heat to low, and simmer 1 hour.

4. Just prior to serving, squeeze juice from half or whole lime into pot and stir well.

5. To serve, sprinkle a handful of tortilla chips over each bowl, then garnish with a dollop of sour cream and some avocado.

Serves 6–8

1 tsp olive oil
1 cup onion, chopped
2 cloves garlic, chopped
2 cups cooked chicken breast, shredded
1 cup frozen corn kernels
1/4 cup dry white wine
1 small can (4 1/2 oz) green chiles, drained
1 tsp ground cumin
1 tsp Worcestershire sauce
1/2 tsp chile powder
2 14 1/2-oz cans no-salt-added chicken broth
1 can peeled and diced tomatoes, undrained
1 10 3/4-oz can tomato soup, undiluted
juice of 1 lime
1 1/4 cups baked unsalted tortilla chips, crushed
sour cream
fresh avocado, diced

Cincinnati-style Chili

1. Simmer meat, onions, and garlic in large stew pot over low heat. Meat should lose its red color but not be overcooked while vegetables soften. Stir frequently about 15 minutes. Spoon off and discard excess fat.

2. Add stock, water, tomato sauce, vinegar, Worcestershire sauce, and bay leaf. Stir well about 5 minutes, keeping heat low. Add chile powder, cumin, oregano, paprika, salt, pepper, cinnamon stick, and chocolate. Stir until everything is mixed well and chocolate has melted in. Add beans and mix well.

3. Simmer 1 1/2 hours, stirring occasionally so chili doesn't scald on bottom of pot. Add water if it seems to be getting too thick.

4. Remove bay leaf and cinnamon stick just prior to serving.

5. Serve hot, garnished with a bit of chopped onion and some cheese. (In Cincinnati the chili is served over hot spaghetti.)

Serves 6

2 pounds ground chuck
2 medium onions, diced
3 cloves garlic, diced
2 cups beef stock
1 cup water
1 16-oz can tomato sauce
2 tbsps red wine vinegar
2 tbsps Worcestershire sauce
1 large bay leaf
4 tbsps chile powder
1 tsp ground cumin
1 tsp dried oregano
1 tsp paprika
salt and black pepper, to taste
1 cinnamon stick
1/2 square (1/2-oz) unsweetened chocolate
1 16-oz can kidney beans, drained and rinsed
1 small onion, chopped, for garnish
1 cup grated cheddar cheese, for garnish

O'Rourke's Diner Roasted Plum Tomato Soup

1. Preheat oven to 475 degrees.

2. Halve tomatoes, lay on baking sheet, and generously coat with oil. Sprinkle with oregano, basil, and garlic. Roast until tomatoes are charred around edges. Let cool slightly.

3. Scrape into bowl of food processor. Process until almost completely smooth. Leave a few light chunks and speckled black ones.

4. Sauté onions in oil in large soup or stew pot until translucent. Add wine and stock; stir. Add evaporated milk and ricotta. Whisk until smooth and blended. Add tomato paste to enrich and thicken. If even thicker soup is desired, add more tomato paste.

5. Taste! You may want to add more basil or oregano and black pepper.

6. To serve, sprinkle a few spoonfuls of grated cheese and a dollop of pesto in the middle of each bowl, and serve piping hot.

To make pesto:

1. Pureé all ingredients except oil in bowl of food processor.

2. Pour in oil slowly and mix well.

Note: Pesto may be made up to five days in advance and kept refrigerated.

Serves 6–8

---

40 ripe plum tomatoes
olive oil
dried oregano
dried basil
6 cloves garlic, chopped fine
2 medium onions, diced fine
1 cup burgundy wine
1 quart chicken or vegetable
    stock
1 14-oz can evaporated milk
1 pound ricotta cheese
1 6-oz can tomato paste
black pepper (optional)
1/2 cup grated Parmesan or
    Romano cheese
spinach pesto (see recipe
    left)

Spinach pesto:
1 10-oz bag fresh spinach
1/4 tsp salt
2 cloves garlic
1 tbsp butter
1 cup pine nuts
1 cup grated good-quality
    cheese (Parmesan or
    Romano)
1 cup olive oil

West Taghakanic Diner Pork Cider Stew

- 1/4 cup vegetable oil
- 5 pounds boneless pork, cut into 1-inch cubes
- 1/2 gallon apple cider
- 4 carrots, diced
- 1 large onion, chopped
- 1/2 bunch celery, diced
- 4 large potatoes, cut into bite-size chunks
- cornstarch
- water

1. Heat oil on medium-high in Dutch oven or stockpot; sear meat until most meat is browned. Add cider until it covers meat. Use more or less depending on how much gravy you want.

2. Lower heat to simmer and cover. Cook 1 hour or until meat is tender.

3. Add vegetables; continue to simmer until tender, up to another hour.

4. Thicken, if necessary, by stirring in some pre-mixed cornstarch and water.

Serves 10

Turkey & Vegetable Soup

1. Heat oil in large stew pot over medium heat; toss in turkey pieces. Brown about 5 minutes on all sides but do not burn. Add stock and water; turn heat down very low. Simmer about 30 minutes; skim off and discard fat.

2. Remove turkey pieces with slotted spoon; set aside to cool a bit.

3. Add onion, beans, and potatoes to pot; stir well. Simmer until potatoes are cooked.

4. Shred turkey meat and return to pot to reheat. Discard skin and bones.

5. Add peas; simmer until cooked, 5 minutes or less.

6. Season with salt and pepper. Serve piping hot, garnished with parsley.

Serves 6

2 tbsps vegetable oil
1 raw turkey breast carcass with meat still on bones, chopped into about 4 pieces
6 cups chicken or turkey stock
2 cups water
1/2 large red onion, peeled and finely chopped
2 cups fresh green beans, chopped into pea-size bits
2 white potatoes, peeled and diced
1 cup frozen peas
salt and black pepper, to taste
parsley, chopped, for garnish

Oasis Café French Onion Soup

- 1/2 stick (4 tbsps) unsalted butter
- 4 large yellow onions, diced
- 2 medium red onions, diced
- 2 scallions
- 1/4 cup port wine
- 4 tbsps garlic, minced
- 4 cups beef stock
- 4 cups water
- 2 tbsps Worcestershire sauce
- 1/2 cup grated Parmesan cheese
- day-old french bread slices
- swiss or gruyère cheese, grated

1. Melt butter in large skillet over low heat; sauté onions and scallions. Cook as long as possible to caramelize without burning. Add port in dashes to slow the carmelizing process.

2. Add garlic and sauté about 5 minutes.

3. Warm stock, water, and Worcestershire sauce in large pot. Scrape in onion mixture; stir well. Toss in Parmesan cheese and stir until it melts.

4. To serve, put a slice of bread in soup bowl, ladle soup over it, and sprinkle with a handful of swiss cheese.

Serves 4

Carrot Sweet Potato Soup

1. Melt butter in large pot. Add onions and ginger, cover, and cook over low heat until tender, about 25 minutes. Add carrots, sweet potatoes, and stock. Bring to a boil.

2. Reduce heat, cover, and simmer until carrots are very tender, about 45 minutes.

3. Pureé soup in batches in blender.

4. Return soup to pot; add orange juice, salt, pepper, ginger, nutmeg, and orange zest, if using, until heated through.

5. Sprinkle each serving with a little freshly ground nutmeg and croutons.

Serves 4–6

4 tbsps butter
2 cups yellow onions, finely chopped
1/4 cup fresh ginger, minced
12 (1 1/2 to 2 pounds) large carrots, peeled and chopped
2 large sweet potatoes, peeled and diced into 1-inch pieces
4 cups chicken stock
1 cup fresh orange juice
salt, black pepper, ground ginger, and ground nutmeg, to taste
fresh orange zest, grated (optional)
fresh nutmeg, grated
large croutons

Butternut Squash & Apple Soup

1. Cook bacon in large pan. Drain on paper towels and crumble. Reserve 1 1/2 teaspoons fat in pan.

2. Add onion, leeks, garlic, bay leaf, salt, and pepper to reserved fat, stirring to soften. Add squash, apple, broth, and water. Simmer, covered, 15 minutes or until squash is tender. Discard bay leaf.

3. Pureé soup in blender and return to saucepan. Add water if too thick.

4. Whisk in crème fraîche, salt, and pepper. Heat on medium-low. Do not boil.

5. To serve, ladle into bowls and sprinkle crumbled bacon on top.

Serves 4

2 slices bacon
1/2 medium onion, chopped fine
1 cup leeks, white and pale green parts washed, chopped fine
1 clove garlic, minced
1/2 bay leaf
salt and black pepper to taste, divided
3 cups (1 1/4 pounds) butternut squash, chopped into 1-inch pieces
1 medium Granny Smith apple, chopped
2 cups chicken broth
1/2 cup water
2 tbsps sour cream or crème fraîche

Edna's Texas Chili

1. Remove casings from sausages and discard. Cut sausages into bite-size pieces; set aside.

2. Heat oil in large pot over medium heat. Sauté onion a few minutes. Add garlic. Do not let vegetables burn.

3. Lower heat to simmer when vegetables are soft. Add cumin and stir well. Add meat, stirring and chopping it with wooden spoon. Add sausages and stir.

4. Cook meats 5–10 minutes until no longer red but not overdone. Stir in tomatoes, vinegar, Worcestershire sauce, and coffee. Stir well. Drizzle in molasses and stir well.

5. Simmer chili 1–2 hours on very low heat, stirring occasionally. Add salt and pepper and more molasses if desired. Add water if chili seems to be getting too thick.

6. Stir in beans about 10 minutes before serving; heat through.

7. Add masa harina paste about 5 minutes before serving to thicken chili and add flavor.

Serves 6

4 hot Italian sausages
1 tbsp olive oil
1 large onion, diced
3 cloves garlic, minced
1 tsp ground cumin
1 pound ground chuck
1 28-oz can crushed tomatoes
1 tsp cider vinegar
1 tsp Worcestershire sauce
4 tbsps strong leftover coffee
1 tsp dark molasses
2 15.5-oz cans kidney beans
1 or 2 tbsps masa harina flour, mixed with water to form paste

Salads & Sides

Among side dishes, the potato rules them all. Cole slaw comes with seafood, and we always encourage eating green vegetables, but in America nothing comes close to the consumption of potatoes, mostly as french fries. Mashed potatoes, however, seem to present one of the greater challenges in the diner industry, and too many use the instant kind. Though we acknowledge the advancement of instant potato technology in the past couple of decades, we contend that you will never, ever find a brand that matches the taste and consistency of an authentic tuber. We can only blame ourselves, of course. Instant potatoes exist because most restaurant patrons have resigned themselves to eating them. With the advent of automatic potato peelers and the relative ease of storage, however, we see no reason for shortcuts.

The side dish puts a personal stamp on the most mundane of meals. Why not a little Mexican flavor added to the rice that's served with meatloaf? A little hot sauce perks up just about anything!

Our favorite side dish is probably the most nutritionally deficient: onion rings. We thank the diner gods for giving us a recipe like Ken's Onion Rings. We thought the art of making true onion rings had vanished under a mountain of the too-perfectly-round, frozen variety. We enjoy the struggle of eating the crusty-but-delicious mess of handmade rings. All things in moderation, we often hear, but a little slip here and there — with ketchup — can't hurt.

Chicken-Walnut-Grape Salad

1. Blend mayonnaise, mustard, and thyme in large mixing bowl. Add chicken; stir to coat well. Add celery and walnuts, mixing well.

2. Stir in grapes and parsley, using wooden spoon.

3. Add remaining 1 tablespoon mayonnaise if salad seems too dry.

4. Chill before serving.

Serves 4

1/2 cup plus 1 tbsp
    mayonnaise, divided
1 tbsp Dijon mustard
1 tsp dried thyme
2 cups white meat chicken,
    cooked, cooled,
    and shredded
3 ribs celery, diced
3/4 cup walnut pieces
1 cup seedless green
    grapes, halved
1/4 cup fresh parsley,
    chopped fine

Savory Potato Salad

1. Cook bacon strips until crisp; drain on paper towels. When cool, tear into 1-inch pieces.

2. Boil potatoes and bay leaf until potatoes are cooked but not mushy. Drain, cool, and chop into 1-inch dice. Discard bay leaf.

3. Place potatoes and bacon in large bowl. Stir in celery, onion, and parsley.

4. Mix mayonnaise, mustard, thyme, and savory in small bowl until well blended. Add salt and pepper.

5. Ladle mayonnaise mixture over potato mixture; stir well with wooden spoon until everything is coated.

6. Chill before serving.

Serves 4

6 pieces bacon
6 red potatoes, unpeeled
1 bay leaf
2 ribs celery, diced
1/2 cup red onion, diced
1/2 cup fresh parsley, diced
1/2 cup mayonnaise
2 tbsps Dijon mustard
1 tsp dried thyme
1 tsp dried summer savory
salt and black pepper,
    to taste

Hoppin' John Rice

1. Cook bacon in large pot until fairly crisp. Drain on paper towels, cool, and break into small pieces.

2. Sauté onions and celery in 3 tablespoons bacon grease over medium heat about 5 minutes. Discard remaining grease. Add garlic near the end so it doesn't overcook.

3. Pour in water; add beans, rice, bay leaf, celery leaves, salt, and pepper. Bring briefly to a boil, reduce heat to a low simmer, cover, and cook about 20 minutes or until rice is done. Discard bay leaf and celery leaves.

4. Serve in soup bowls; scatter bacon bits over top.

Serves 4–6

4 pieces hickory-smoked
    bacon
3 medium onions, diced
2 ribs celery, diced
2 cloves garlic, minced
4 cups water
2 16-oz cans black-eyed
    peas, drained
1 cup long-grain white rice
1 bay leaf
few celery leaves
salt and black pepper,
    to taste

Ken's Onion Rings

1. Peel and slice onions to 1/8- to 1/4-inch thick. Put in large bowl; pour milk over them (keeps them firm, white, and moist).

2. Mix equal amounts flour and bread crumbs in separate bowl until well blended. Stir in salt and pepper.

3. Swish heaping handful of onions in flour-bread crumb mixture until coated. Shake off excess.

4. Deep-fry in hot, clean oil, stirring occasionally until crispy golden brown.

5. Drain on paper towels, blot a bit, and serve hot.

Serves 10–12

5 large whole Spanish
   onions
2 cups milk
white flour
plain bread crumbs
salt and black pepper,
   to taste
oil

Real Mashed Potatoes

1. Boil potatoes in lightly salted water until tender but not mushy. Check with fork or sharp knife. Keep pan loosely covered.

2. Drain in colander; return to pot. Increase heat to medium and toss potatoes until excess moisture is gone. Turn off heat, cover, and let sit a few minutes.

3. Heat half-and-half in small saucepan, taking care not to scald.

4. Pour half-and-half and melted butter over still-warm potatoes. Sprinkle in salt and pepper. Mash briefly just to blend.

5. With mixer whip potatoes on medium to high speed until smooth. Taste and adjust seasonings. Serve at once.

Serves 4

5 large baking potatoes,
   peeled and cut into
   quarters
1/2 cup half-and-half
3 tbsps butter, melted
salt and freshly ground
   white pepper, to taste

Tuna Salad Niçoise

1. Cook potatoes in lightly salted boiling water until fork-tender, about 10 minutes. Put potatoes in large bowl using slotted spoon. Reserve cooking water.

2. Whisk vinaigrette; pour about 1/3 over potatoes. Toss to coat, then let cool. Cut in half if potatoes are large.

3. Boil potato water, toss in beans, and cook 2 minutes. Drain in colander; rinse with cold water to stop the cooking process and preserve color. Cool.

4. Arrange lettuce leaves on plates or serving platter. Put a scoop of tuna in middle of each leaf. Array potatoes, green beans, tomatoes, and olives around tuna.

5. Sprinkle onion on top of tuna to resemble confetti.

6. Dip eggs in parsley and place around tuna.

7. Add capers to remaining vinaigrette just before serving, whisk well, and drizzle over everything.

To make vinaigrette:

Whisk all ingredients together. Let sit 1 hour.

Serves 4

1 pound red-skinned new
     potatoes, unpeeled
vinaigrette (see recipe
     left), divided
1/2 pound fresh green beans,
     ends trimmed off
1 head romaine lettuce,
     leaves separated
2 small (6-oz) cans tuna,
     drained
12 cherry tomatoes
1/2 cup niçoise olives
1/2 red onion, minced
4 hard-boiled eggs,
     quartered
3 tbsps parsley, minced
1 tbsp capers, drained

Vinaigrette:
3 tbsps red wine vinegar
8 tbsps olive oil
4 tbsps vegetable oil
1/2 tsp dried thyme
1/2 tsp dried rosemary
1/2 tsp dried summer savory
1/2 tsp salt
1/4 tsp red pepper flakes
1/4 tsp black pepper

Teddy Joe's Mexican Rice

1. Rinse rice and let dry 1 hour.

2. Heat oil in large skillet over medium; toss in rice to coat. Add cumin and oregano; stir well. Cook a few minutes; reduce heat.

3. Add onions, carrots, green pepper, corn, and garlic. Mix after each addition. Cook a few minutes. Add tomatoes and stir well.

4. Raise heat; stir in liquid. It will steam. Cover pan quickly; let sit about 3 minutes. Remove lid, lower heat to low simmer, and stir in cilantro, salt, and pepper. Cover skillet again.

5. Simmer 30–45 minutes or until rice absorbs liquid and is cooked.

Serves 6

1 cup long-grain white rice
1 green bell pepper, diced
1 medium onion, diced
1 cup carrots, peeled
    and diced
2 cloves garlic, minced
1 28-oz can whole peeled
    tomatoes, cut into
    quarters, liquid reserved
1 tbsp oil
2 tsp ground cumin
1 tsp dried oregano
1 cup corn (fresh or frozen,
    not canned)
reserved tomato liquid and
    water to equal 3 cups
1 small bunch fresh cilantro,
    chopped into bits
salt and black pepper,
    to taste

Sarah's Dinner Rolls

1. Dissolve yeast in water about 5 minutes until it begins to bubble.

2. Scald milk in saucepan; add sugar and salt. Remove from heat.

3. Add butter and let melt, slightly cooling mixture. Add eggs and mix.

4. Put egg mixture in large bowl; mix in some flour. Add yeast mixture. Add more flour while kneading until soft dough comes clean from your hands.

5. Let rise in a warm place until dough has doubled, about 90 minutes.

6. Punch down, letting air escape.

7. Preheat oven to 375 degrees.

8. Shape into individual rolls (Parker house, snails, cloverleaf, or rosettes), using about 1/2 cup dough for each. Bake on ungreased cookie sheets for about 15 minutes or until browned.

Makes about 24 rolls

1 pkg dry yeast
1/2 cup warm water
1 cup milk
1/2 cup sugar
1 tsp salt
1 stick (1/2 cup) cold butter,
    cut in pieces
2 eggs, beaten frothy
5 or more cups unbleached
    white flour

Ted's Double-Butter Biscuits

1. Preheat oven to 450 degrees.

2. Using fork, mix flour, sugar, salt, baking powder, and baking soda in large bowl. Cut in butter until mixture looks like coarse meal. Stir in buttermilk a little at a time until dough is pliable but not too sticky.

3. Put dough on lightly floured board and knead lightly about 20 times. Roll to about 1/2-inch thick. Cut biscuits with floured biscuit cutter, glass, or jelly jar.

4. Place biscuits on two ungreased cookie sheets; bake 10–12 minutes or until golden brown.

Makes about 18 biscuits

2 cups unbleached flour
1/2 tsp sugar
1/2 tsp salt
1 1/2 tsps baking powder
1 tsp baking soda
1/3 cup butter, chilled
2/3 cup buttermilk

Donna's Cold Macaroni Salad

1. Cook macaroni according to package instructions. Drain and place in large bowl to cool.

2. Pour whisked vinaigrette over cooled macaroni. Stir well to coat. Add onion, celery, olives, and parsley; mix well with wooden spoon. Stir in sour cream to bind ingredients.

3. Chill at least 1 hour before serving.

2 cups elbow macaroni
vinaigrette (see recipe right)
1 small onion, diced
2 ribs celery, diced
1/2 cup stuffed olives,
    chopped
1 small bunch parsley,
    chopped small
3 tbsps sour cream

Vinaigrette:
2 tbsps red wine vinegar
1 tbsp vegetable oil

To make vinaigrette:

Whisk ingredients together well.

Serves 4

Garlicky Salad Dressing

Note: This recipe contains raw eggs.

1. Blend all ingredients except oil in blender or food processor.

2. Drizzle in oil while still blending until desired thickness is reached and ingredients are smooth and well blended.

3. Keep refrigerated; whisk just before using.

Makes about 1 cup

1/2 cup red wine vinegar
2 eggs
2 tbsps garlic, minced
pinch dried tarragon
pinch dried thyme
salt and white pepper,
    to taste
olive oil

Ranch Salad Dressing

- 1 cup mayonnaise
- 1/4 tsp dried chives
- 1/4 tsp dried parsley
- 1/4 tsp dried oregano
- 1/4 tsp garlic powder
- 2 tsps onion salt
- 1/4 tsp white pepper
- 1 cup buttermilk

1. Mix all ingredients except buttermilk in blender until smooth. Drizzle in buttermilk and continue to blend a few minutes.

2. Refrigerate in covered container overnight.

3. Just before serving, stir well.

Makes 4–5 cups

Corn Relish

1. Blend onion, cilantro, and pimento in blender or food processor. Be careful not to purée.

2. Scrape into mixing bowl, add corn, and stir well. Squeeze in lime juice and mix well. Add salt and pepper.

3. Cover and refrigerate until ready to use.

Serves 4

1 small red onion, chopped
1 small bunch cilantro,
    chopped
4 pieces pimento, chopped
1 cup corn, cooked
    (or canned, drained)
juice of 1 lime
salt and white pepper,
    to taste

Marinated Onions

These are great on burgers, sandwiches, and in salads.

1. Peel and slice onions by hand. Place in glass bowl or jar.

2. Pour in sugar, cover, and shake to coat. Pour in enough vinegar to submerge onions.

3. Let sit at room temperature a few hours or until onions are shocking pink.

Makes 4–5 cups

4 large red onions
1/2 cup sugar
white vinegar

Julie's Mushroom-Barley Ragout

1. Heat oil in large nonstick pot and sauté onions and garlic until translucent, about 10 minutes. Add mushrooms, bell pepper, sage, and cayenne; continue sautéing, stirring frequently, until mushrooms are wilted, about 1 minute. Add wine, stock, water, Worcestershire sauce, and bay leaves. Bring mixture to a boil.

2. Add barley and lower heat. Simmer uncovered until barley is tender, 35–40 minutes.

3. Taste stew while it cooks. If wine taste is too heavy, add sugar a little at a time to cut acidity. If it seems too thick, add more water or stock.

4. When barley is fully cooked, add peas, cheese, and salt; cook just enough to melt cheese into stew and heat peas.

Serves 6

1 tbsp olive oil
3 medium onions, chopped
5 cloves garlic, minced
at least 1 1/2 pounds
    fresh mushrooms
1 red bell pepper, chopped
2 tbsps fresh sage, chopped,
    or 1 tsp dried
1/2 tsp cayenne
2 cups dry red wine
3 cups chicken or
    vegetable stock
1 cup water
splash Worcestershire sauce
2 bay leaves
1 cup pearl barley
1 to 2 tsps sugar (optional)
1 cup frozen baby peas
4 oz low-fat goat cheese or
    ricotta (optional)
salt, to taste

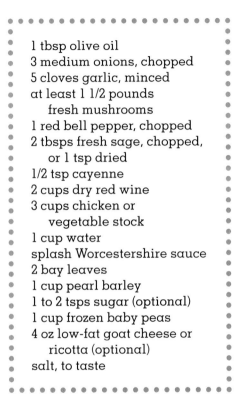

Cucumber Salad

1. Peel cucumbers; cut into thin slices and dice.

2. Toss cucumbers in large bowl with vinaigrette until coated. Let sit 5 minutes, toss again, and drain off liquid. Add tomatoes, onion, and dill; stir well. Pour on yogurt or sour cream; mix well.

3. Chill before serving.

Serves 4

2 cucumbers, about
    8 inches long
vinaigrette (see recipe right)
12 cherry tomatoes, halved
1 small onion, diced
1 tbsp fresh dill, chopped
1/2 cup plain yogurt or
    sour cream

Vinaigrette:
1/2 tsp salt
2 tsps cider vinegar
1/4 tsp sugar

To make vinaigrette:

Whisk all ingredients together.

Ginger Ale Gelatin Salad

1. Dissolve gelatin in water in large bowl, stirring a bit. Pour in grape juice and stir well. Add sugar, salt, ginger ale, and lemon juice, mixing well after each addition.

2. Refrigerate about 20 minutes until cool.

3. Stir in fruit and ginger.

4. Chill in bowl or ring mold.

Serves 4–6

2 tbsps (1/4-oz packet) gelatin
1/4 cup cold water
1/2 cup white or purple grape juice, boiled
1/2 cup sugar
pinch salt
2 cups ginger ale
juice of 1 lemon
1 cup seedless green or red grapes, halved
1 tangerine, clementine mandarin orange, or orange, peeled and sectioned
2 tsps chopped candied ginger

Ann Sather's Creamed Spinach

1. Cook spinach in water according to package directions, until tender.

2. While spinach is cooking, stir in onion, nutmeg, salt, and pepper.

3. Drain in colander, immediately add to sauce, stir well, and serve piping hot.

Serves 4

1 pound (16 oz) frozen chopped spinach
1/4 cup onion, grated
1 tsp ground nutmeg
1 tsp salt
1/2 tsp black pepper
sauce (see recipe right)

To make sauce:

1. Melt butter in saucepan, stir in flour, and mix vigorously to avoid clumping. Whisk in the milk a little bit at a time.

2. Cook until sauce thickens; stir in salt and pepper.

Sauce:
1/4 cup butter
1/4 cup white flour
1 1/2 cups milk
1 tsp salt
1/4 tsp white pepper

Zucchini Tart

1. Melt butter in large skillet over medium-low heat. Add basil and stir. Add onion. Cook about 5 minutes until onion is soft. Add garlic and cook 1 minute. Add zucchini and sauté until liquid cooks off, about 5 minutes.

2. Preheat oven to 350 degrees.

3. Layer cheese in bottom of pie shell. Spoon zucchini mixture evenly over cheese. Smooth top.

4. Bake about 15 minutes until cheese melts. Serve warm.

Serves 4

3 tbsps butter
1 tsp dried basil or Italian seasoning
1 large onion, diced
1 tbsp garlic, minced
2 1/2 cups zucchini, shredded or grated
1 cup grated mozzarella cheese
1 9-inch baked single crust pie shell

Sandwich Classics

When all else fails, order a sandwich. You simply will not find a more versatile meal on the menu. The Mastoris Diner in Bordentown, New Jersey, for instance, boasts nearly eighty sandwiches on its voluminous menu — a true testament to what can be put between two (or three) slices of bread.

Most diners offer the same core sandwiches. Clubs, kings of this realm, get high marks from just about everyone — except those who must make them. Tuna salad comes cold or in a melt. Chicken salad with lettuce and tomato, along with a nice cup of chicken-and-rice soup, often hits the spot. BLT, grilled cheese, and ham sandwiches round out the classics in any self-respecting diner.

With freshly baked bread, any ordinary sandwich becomes a true culinary treat. At the Parkway Diner in Worcester, Massachusetts, John Evangelista puts savory homemade meatballs between slices of freshly baked Italian bread and creates a truly sublime lunchtime experience. In Jessup, Maryland, Frank and Linda Davis serve up their signature meatloaf sandwich with lettuce, tomato, and a touch of mayo on large slices of whole-grain bread to create one of the best meals you'll ever hold in your hand.

Though everyone has favorites, we name the turkey sandwich as a true diner bench mark as long as it's the real thing — roasted that day and carved right off the bird. Serve it on a fresh roll or wheat bread with any cheese but American, garnish it with lettuce and a fresh tomato slice, and we're smiling well into dinnertime.

Easy BBQ Pork Sandwich

1. Put water, vinegar, bay leaf, and garlic in large saucepan and heat but do not boil.

2. In skillet heat small amount of oil. Sear cutlets on each side (about 1 minute or less per side); remove to a plate.

3. Lower saucepan heat and put cutlets into water mixture. Cook, covered, about 30 minutes or until pork is fork tender. Skim off any fat that accumulates on top.

4. Pour barbeque sauce into skillet and heat on medium-low.

5. Split rolls, butter, and lightly toast.

6. Put one cutlet on each roll and spoon on as much warm sauce as you want. Serve hot with plenty of napkins. Great with cole slaw on the side.

Serves 4

1 cup water
2 tsps cider vinegar
1 bay leaf
1 clove garlic, minced
oil
4 boneless pork cutlets, about 1/4-inch thick
your favorite barbeque sauce
4 kaiser or other bulky rolls
butter

Chicken Club Sandwich

1. Cook bacon until crisp; drain on paper towels.

2. Using a very sharp knife, cut tomatoes into 1/4-inch slices; use three slices per sandwich.

3. Toast bread lightly. When cool, spread with generous amounts of mayonnaise.

4. Cut chicken to desired thickness with sharp knife; sprinkle both sides lightly with salt and pepper. Do not cut chicken until you are ready to use it because it will become dry.

5. To assemble alternate layers: bread, mayonnaise, chicken, tomato, bacon, lettuce, bread. Repeat layers for each sandwich.

6. Cut sandwiches diagonally. If necessary, secure layers with a toothpick or two. Serve with pickle spears and potato chips.

Serves 2

6 slices bacon
2 beefsteak tomatoes
whole-wheat bread
mayonnaise
several pieces white meat
    chicken (ideally breast
    meat), cooked and cooled
salt and black pepper,
    to taste
several pieces crisp, crunchy
    lettuce, such as romaine
    or Bibb

Fried Fish Po' Boy

1. Put oil in bottom of large skillet; turn heat to medium.

2. Mix cornmeal, flour, thyme, cayenne, and salt on plate.

3. Dip fish in milk to coat; dredge in flour mixture. Mixture should stick well.

4. Fry fish in hot but not smoking oil until golden brown and just cooked through, about 5 minutes per side. Remove from pan and set aside.

5. Spoon oil from pan, leaving less than 1 tablespoon. Add garlic and sauté briefly. Squeeze in some lemon juice, to taste, then stir to scrape up browned bits from bottom of pan. Remove pan from heat.

6. Quickly stir mayonnaise into garlic-lemon-oil mixture. Spread on both sides of roll, add fish and lettuce, if using.

Serves 1

2 or 3 tbsps oil
1 tbsp cornmeal
1 tbsp white flour
scant pinch dried thyme
scant pinch cayenne
salt to taste
1 firm fish fillet (catfish, perch, or snapper), skinned
1/4 cup milk
1 small clove garlic, minced
1 lemon, cut into quarters
2 tsps mayonnaise
1 kaiser roll or 1 small baguette
shredded iceberg lettuce (optional)

Ham & Relish Sandwich

1. Spread both slices of bread with cream cheese.

2. Spoon on pickle relish, pressing into cream cheese.

3. Add ham to one slice and put slices together to complete.

Serves 1

good-quality sliced rye,
    pumpernickel, or marbled
    (combo of both) bread
cream cheese, softened to
    room temperature
diced-pickle relish
sliced ham

Italian Sausage & Pepper Hero

1. Preheat oven to 375 degrees.

2. Slice sausages into bite-size pieces. In large saucepan, sauté over medium-low heat 2 minutes. Do not add oil.

3. Pour in wine. Continue to cook, turning sausages occasionally, until all wine cooks off and sausages are brown on all sides, about 10 minutes. Remove and set aside.

4. Add oil to skillet if it is dry and raise heat to medium. Toss in onion and cook about 5 minutes. It may brown a little. Add garlic and herbs, stir well, and cook a few more minutes. Add tomato sauce and stir vigorously to coat everything.

5. Lower heat and add green pepper. Simmer a few minutes until pepper wilts and edges begin to brown.

6. Brush both halves of roll with oil. Put sausages on both halves; spoon vegetable mixture over everything.

7. Press sandwiches together and wrap in aluminum foil. Place on cookie sheet and warm in oven 5–10 minutes. Unwrap, sprinkle with cheese, and serve with lots of napkins.

Serves 2

2 sweet Italian sausages
1/4 cup red wine
1 tbsp olive oil
1/4 onion, sliced thin
1 clove garlic, minced
pinch each dried basil, dried oregano, and red pepper flakes
1 tbsp tomato sauce
1 green bell pepper, seeded, membrane removed, sliced thin
1 long crusty roll, halved
grated Parmesan cheese

Cape Ann Lobster-Salad Roll

1. In large bowl whisk shallots, tarragon, a squeeze or two of lemon (to taste), and vinegar.

2. Add celery and toss to coat.

3. Stir in lobster pieces. Let stand 5 minutes to marinate.

4. Add a little mayonnaise, mixing well after each addition. Salad should be just moistened, not gloppy.

5. Toast and lightly butter rolls. Spoon lobster mixture onto rolls and serve.

Serves 6

1 tsp shallots, minced
1 tbsp fresh tarragon (or
    1 1/2 tbsp dried)
1 lemon, cut into quarters
2 tbsp white vinegar
2 ribs celery, diced
    very small
3 cups cooked lobster meat,
    broken into 1-inch or
    smaller chunks
1/2 to 3/4 cup mayonnaise
6 good-quality hot dog rolls
    or similar
butter

Philly-style Cheesesteak

1. Preheat broiler.

2. Melt some butter in saucepan over low heat; add onion. Sauté until soft, about 5 minutes. Do not brown. Turn off heat, add salt and pepper, and toss. Stir in mustard.

3. Slice rolls in half lengthwise, butter lightly, and toast briefly under broiler. Remove, cool slightly, and spread with onion-mustard mixture. Spoon on pan juices, if desired.

4. Set bottom halves on cookie sheet or in large pan. Lay beef on each piece and top with cheese. Place under broiler a few seconds until cheese melts.

5. Replace tops, cut sandwiches in half, and serve.

Serves 2

butter
1 small onion, sliced thin
salt and black pepper, to taste
1 tsp Dijon mustard
2 hero or other big sandwich rolls
1/2 pound or more shredded chip steak (super-thin sandwich steaks or roast beef)
6 or more slices American, mild cheddar, or Muenster cheese

Sloppy Joes

1. Sauté chuck and onion over moderately high heat, stirring until meat is no longer pink and is separated.

2. Lower heat, add remaining ingredients except buns, and cook 30 minutes.

3. To serve, split open a bun, scoop a generous serving of chuck mixture on bottom half, and replace top half.

Serves 4

- 1 pound ground chuck
- 1/2 cup chopped onion
- 1/2 cup chopped bell pepper
- 1 cup canned crushed tomatoes
- 1 tbsp white vinegar
- 1 tbsp fresh lemon juice
- 1 tbsp Worcestershire sauce
- 1 tsp Dijon mustard
- 1 tsp paprika
- 1 tbsp dark brown sugar
- hamburger buns

Turkey & Cranberry Sandwich

1. Spread both slices of bread with thin coating of mayonnaise.

2. Lightly salt and pepper turkey; add to one slice.

3. Spoon cranberry relish onto turkey and top with lettuce. Add second slice to complete.

To make relish:

Boil all ingredients, cool, and refrigerate for an hour or until it jells.

Serves 1

2 slices good-quality white
    sandwich bread
mayonnaise
sliced cooked turkey,
    preferably white meat
salt and black pepper,
    to taste
cranberry relish (see recipe
    left)
one or two leaves romaine
    lettuce

Relish:
1 cup cranberries
1/2 tsp lemon zest
1 cup sugar
1 tsp fresh ginger, grated

Ham, Tomato, & Egg Sandwich

1. Lightly butter two slices of bread.

2. Mix dressing and spread on both slices.

3. Layer on ham, tomato, and egg. Add lettuce.

To make dressing:

Mix all ingredients together well.

Serves 1

butter
2 slices rye bread
dressing (see recipe left)
sliced ham
1 beefsteak tomato, sliced
    1/4-inch thick
1 hard-boiled egg, sliced
    1/4-inch thick
lettuce

Dressing:
1 tbsp mayonnaise
1/4 tsp jarred horseradish

Meatloaf Sandwich

1. Slice meatloaf to desired thickness.

2. Lay a slice or two of cheese atop each piece; warm briefly in microwave or toaster oven until cheese melts.

3. To make sandwich, put meatloaf-cheese on first slice of bread, sprinkle onions on top, and add second slice of bread.

Serves 1

leftover meatloaf, sliced
sliced cheese (American is
    best)
canned fried onions
2 slices white sandwich
    bread

Bob's Diner
134 Lancaster Avenue — Route U. S. 30
Columbia, Penna.

Bellevue Diner
Located at Montgomeryville, Pa.
on Route U S 309

"WHERE FOOD ATTAINS PERFECTION"

COURT HOUSE CAFE - Effingham, Illinois

Grilled to Perfection

Of all the diners we love, those with their grills out front with the customers we love the most. You'll find no better show than a grill man deftly preparing a half-dozen orders or more right before your eyes. At the epicenter of the action, a seasoned grill man hears everything, meets everyone, and sets the tone of the operation. Stop in at the Capitol Diner in Lynn, Massachusetts, and a few words with the grill man might even lead to legislation, because Bobby Fennel not only owns this landmark diner but also is a state representative.

The diner was designed to be operated by a mere handful of people to cook, serve, and bus. An owner who also worked the grill could see first-hand every aspect of the operation. Customers had a direct line to the chief, and employees, who often included family members, always remained under the watchful eye of the boss.

When operations became larger, problems arose. Some diners complained that customers often bypassed the waitress and placed orders directly with the grill man. Grilled specialties joined side dishes and soups on the growing menus; more complex meals required a deeper integration with the rest of the "line." Responsibilities had to be delegated. The best way to keep control of the work flow was to isolate the cook in the kitchen. Thus, by the 1950s owners had become more concerned with efficiency than with theater, moved grills into the kitchens, and, sadly, deprived customers of a cheap source of entertainment.

Duplicating the magic at home may take a professional grill, which some people have in their kitchens. For the rest of us, we suggest using seasoned cast iron skillets, real butter, and a general abandonment of so-called lite cuisine. Enjoy yourself, and remember why we still call it comfort food. The good feeling you get from the experience has its own health benefits.

Pan-fried Fish Fillet

1. Wash fillets in cold water and pat dry with paper towels, then set on a plate until needed.

2. Melt butter in skillet over medium-high heat until bubbling but not browning.

3. Pour flour onto a plate.

4. Liberally salt and pepper both sides of fillets. Dredge in flour, shake off excess, and immediately place in skillet. Sear about 1 minute on each side. Turn carefully with large spatula to keep fillet intact. Lower heat to simmer; cover skillet. Cook 2 or 3 more minutes per side.

5. Fillets are done when springy to the touch. Squeeze lemon juice on top and serve at once.

Serves 2

2 firm white fish fillets, such
    as sole, halibut, or cod
butter
1/2 cup white flour
salt and black pepper,
    to taste
1 lemon, quartered

Unadilla Diner Fruit Crepes

1. In large bowl mix flour and sugar well. Whisk in milk and water; blend until very smooth.

2. In small bowl blend egg, egg yolk, butter, and salt.

3. Add egg mixture to flour mixture and mix thoroughly. Put in refrigerator; chill 1 hour. When ready to use, whisk well.

4. Heat heavy-duty nonstick skillet; melt enough butter to coat bottom well.

5. Pour about 1/4 cup batter in center of pan and immediately tilt pan in all directions to form round flat crepe. Cook only about 30 seconds, then quickly flip and cook other side no more than 30 seconds. Place on cake-cooling rack rather than plate to cool without getting moist.

6. Preheat oven to 250 degrees.

7. To fill crepes, lightly butter top side, spoon on filling, and roll. Put on cookie sheet and warm in oven a few minutes.

8. To serve, dust with powdered sugar and offer vanilla ice cream or whipped cream.

Serves 6

1/2 cup white flour
1 tsp sugar
1/4 cup milk
1/4 cup water
1 large egg plus 1 egg yolk
1 1/2 tbsps butter, melted
1/4 tsp salt
butter
fruit filling of choice
powdered sugar
ice cream or real
    whipped cream

Triangle Diner, Folsom, New Jersey

DINER

Gus & Louie's Ultimate Home Fries

1. For best results, use a black cast iron skillet; heat over medium. Pour 2 tablespoons oil into pan.

2. While oil is heating, peel, wash, and dry potatoes. Cut into random shapes; variation adds character. Each piece should be about ice-cube size.

3. Lift and tilt pan to spread oil evenly. Add potatoes.

4. With spatula immediately turn potatoes. Continue turning until they are coated on all sides. Sprinkle paprika, oregano, salt, and a couple of shakes of pepper over potatoes. Turn often to brown evenly. Don't leave potatoes unattended; browning takes only 8–10 minutes.

5. When potatoes are brown, hold pan lid in one hand. With other hand add 1 tablespoon water and immediately cover pan. When steam stops escaping (about 1 minute, no more!), lift lid and cut one or two potatoes with spatula. If potatoes are still hard, repeat steaming process another minute.

6. When potatoes are done, use spatula to get under potatoes (don't push them); move them to perimeter of pan.

7. Add remaining 1 teaspoon oil to middle of pan; drop onion on top of oil. Turn off heat.

8. Cook only 1 minute while turning onions. Mix potatoes and onions together, add olive oil, mix again, and bank them against side of pan. Don't cover. Serve hot.

Serves 4

- 2 tbsps plus 1 tsp canola or corn oil, divided
- 4 4-inch by 2-inch Maine potatoes
- 1 tsp paprika
- 1 tsp dried oregano
- 1/2 tsp salt
- freshly ground black pepper, to taste
- 1 tbsp water
- 1 cup sweet onion (Vidalia preferred), coarsely chopped
- 1 tsp olive oil

Chicken-fried Steak with Country Gravy

1. Make gravy and keep warm until needed.

2. In large bowl mix buttermilk, Tabasco sauce, and pepper.

3. On large plate mix flour, cayenne, and marjoram.

4. Heat equal parts oil and butter in frying pan.

5. Pound meat with mallet until doubled. Dredge first in buttermilk mixture then in flour mixture, shaking off excess.

6. Fry until golden brown, frying first side well before turning. Remove from pan and blot with paper towel.

7. Pour hot gravy over meat and serve at once.

Serves 2–4

gravy (see recipe right)
1 cup buttermilk
2 tbsps Tabasco sauce
pinch white pepper
2 cups white flour
2 tbsps cayenne
1 tbsp dried marjoram
1 tbsp oil
1 tbsp unsalted butter
1 pound flank steak

Gravy:
1 cup milk
1/2 cup chicken stock
1 pimento, chopped
2 tbsps ground black pepper

To make gravy:

In a large saucepan over medium heat, stir the ingredients together. Heat, but do not allow to boil.

Church Dinner Swiss Steak

1. On large plate mix flour with salt and pepper. Coat meat, shaking off excess.

2. In large skillet heat butter and oil together. Add meat and brown on all sides. Use slotted spoon and remove meat to warm plate.

3. Lower heat and sauté onions, celery, and garlic about 5 minutes or until they begin to soften. Stir in thyme, sugar, and tomatoes. Simmer a few minutes.

4. Return meat and any juices to pan. Add wine and broth; simmer until meat is quite tender, about 1 hour.

5. Skim off any fat, add salt and pepper, and serve hot.

Serves 4–6

1/4 cup white flour
salt and black pepper, to taste, divided
2 pounds chuck steak, cut into cubes
1 tbsp butter
1 tbsp oil
4 medium onions, sliced thin
1 celery rib, diced
2 cloves garlic, minced
1 1/2 tsps dried thyme
1/2 tsp sugar
1 16-oz can crushed tomatoes
1/2 cup dry red wine
1/2 cup canned beef broth

Georgia's Chicken & Onion Fricassee

1. Heat butter in large skillet over medium-low.

2. Salt and pepper chicken pieces and sauté in pan until golden, not browned.

3. Using a slotted spoon, remove smaller pieces of chicken. Add onions, cover, and simmer no more than 5 minutes.

4. Return reserved chicken pieces to pan; add wine and stock. Stir to coat. Bring to a boil, lower heat to simmer, cover pan, and cook 15–20 minutes.

5. Using the slotted spoon, remove all chicken and most onions to a bowl.

6. Raise heat and reduce sauce to about 1 cup, stirring constantly. Add mushrooms and cream; cook 5 minutes to soften mushrooms and thicken sauce further.

7. Return chicken and onions to pan to reheat. Serve hot over noodles.

Serves 4–6

4 tbsps butter
salt and black pepper, to taste
1 3-pound chicken, skin on, cut into 6 or 8 pieces
2 medium onions, diced
1 cup white wine
1/2 chicken stock or canned broth
3 cups mushrooms, cleaned and sliced thin
1 cup light cream

Calf's Liver with Onions & Soused Raisins

1. In small bowl soak raisins in bourbon.

2. In large skillet melt about half of the oil and butter, and heat. Toss in onions and cook until they begin to carmelize, 10–15 minutes. Remove with slotted spoon and set aside.

3. On plate mix flour with salt and pepper. Dredge liver and shake off excess.

4. Add the remaining oil and butter to pan, increase heat, and cook liver until both sides are browned but still pink inside, about 5 minutes. Remove to another plate.

5. Drain raisins; in same skillet reduce heat to medium and cook raisins, vinegar, and spices, scraping and reducing.

6. To serve, spoon onions and raisin sauce over liver.

Serves 2–4

1/4 cup raisins
3 tsps bourbon
2 tbsps oil, divided
3 tsps butter, divided
3 medium onions, sliced thin and chopped
4 tbsps white flour
salt and black pepper, to taste
1 pound calf's liver, cut into 8 slices
2 tbsps red wine vinegar
ground cloves and ground nutmeg, to taste

Dulce's Gloucester-style Fish Cakes

1. In large bowl mix parsley, onion, eggs, garlic powder, salt, and pepper.

2. Add potatoes and cod; mix well. Add a small amount of flour if batter is too thin.

3. Heat oil in large skillet over medium.

4. Use two tablespoons to shape batter into oval cakes. Place cakes in hot oil and fry until golden brown. Drain on paper towels.

Serves 4–6

1/4 cup parsley, finely chopped
1 medium onion, finely chopped
4 eggs
1 tsp garlic powder
salt and black pepper, to taste
5 medium potatoes, cooked and mashed
1 to 1 1/2 pounds fresh cod, boiled and shredded
white flour
2 tbsps corn oil

Alison's Diner Turkey Burger

1. Shape turkey into burger-type patty; salt and pepper both sides.

2. Heat small frying pan over medium-high until hot enough to sear. Add oil, swirl to coat pan, and immediately add burger.

3. Fry until patty is well browned, flip over, and brown other side, reducing heat slightly and cook until juice starts to rise out of top of burger. Remove from pan and keep warm.

4. Cook garlic in pan juices until garlic starts to brown. Turn heat to high, toss in tomatoes, and cook, stirring fairly constantly, until pieces turn to mush and reduce slightly.

5. Pour over burger and serve immediately.

Serves 1

about 1/4 pound
    ground turkey
salt and black pepper,
    to taste
2 tbsps olive oil
6 large cloves garlic,
    coarsely chopped
12 cherry tomatoes,
    quartered

Cheese-stuffed Hamburgers

1. In large skillet melt oil and butter over medium heat; sauté onion a few minutes until soft. Set aside.

2. Form eight thin hamburger patties. Spoon onions on top center of four patties. Add about 1 tablespoon cheese on top of onions; press into place.

3. Place plain patties over prepared ones, sealing in toppings by pinching edges all around.

4. Turn heat to medium and pan-sauté until well browned on each side but not overcooked.

5. Serve on buns.

Serves 4

l tsp vegetable oil
l tsp butter
l medium onion, sliced very thin
l pound lean ground chuck
4 tbsps cheese, grated or crumbled (sharp cheddar, swiss, or even Gorgonzola), divided
4 good-quality hamburger buns, toasted

Skirt Steak Fajita

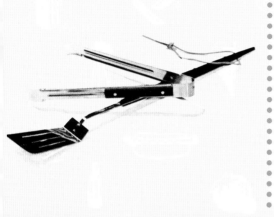

1 tbsp lime juice
1 tbsp vegetable oil
1 pound skirt steak (or thin
    sirloin)
salt and black pepper, to
    taste
4 large flour tortillas
1 cup shredded Monterey
    Jack cheese
salsa
guacamole
sour cream

1. In large ceramic bowl, whisk lime juice and oil.

2. Using a very sharp knife, cut meat into about 4-inch-long thin pieces. Sprinkle well with salt and pepper; marinate in lime juice mixture 15 minutes at room temperature.

3. Preheat oven to 250 degrees; warm tortillas on cookie sheet.

4. Heat skillet over medium-high. Sear meat on both sides, lower heat a bit, and cook a few minutes until medium-rare.

5. To assemble, place a tortilla on each plate and spoon on salsa and guacamole. Ladle on meat. Sprinkle on some pan juices if desired, but don't overdo it or fajitas will be soggy. Scatter cheese over everything, roll up tortilla, top with a dollop of sour cream, and serve.

Serves 2

More Blue Plate Specials

Sometime in the early 1990s, a publication called *The Whole Pop Catalog* explained the origins of the blue plate special. It cited stories of diners in New York and Chicago that served meals on partitioned blue plastic plates made during the Depression. Because a source wasn't cited, we regard the story with some suspicion, especially because plastic did not come into widespread use until well after World War II.

In 2002 food connoisseur and historian Daniel Rogov put forth what seems to be the definitive answer: The term first appeared on the menus of the famous Fred Harvey restaurants.

Fred Harvey restaurants were in many train stations along the Santa Fe railroad. The restaurants served both the itinerant and fast-moving passenger trade – on blue ceramic plates Mr. Harvey ordered from a company in Illinois. The term *blue plate special* was first seen on Fred Harvey menus in 1892, and it referred to meals his restaurants could serve within the 15 minutes passengers usually had between trains. Given Harvey's seminal role in the development of our fast-food industry, we give this theory the most credence.

Aside from all the debate on the term's origins, few will deny the appeal of a good hot meal at a discount. Traditionally, blue plate specials mean meatloaf, mac and cheese, or another common, easy-to-make, rib-sticking meal. Rarely, if ever, have we seen it served on a blue plate, but why be picky in the face of such an appetizing experience? Just pass the pepper.

Franny's American Chop Suey

1. Heat oil in large skillet and brown pork well; set aside.

2. Sauté mushrooms; set aside.

3. Brown onion, garlic, and celery well. Return meat and mushrooms to skillet and add broth, stirring well to scrape up bits from bottom of pan. Add bean sprouts, water chestnuts, and bamboo shoots; season with soy sauce and additional seasonings, if desired. Heat through; simmer about 30 minutes.

4. Serve over cooked rice.

Serves 4–6

1 tbsp oil
1 pound pork shoulder, cut
  up for stew
1/2 pound mushrooms,
  sliced thin
1 onion, sliced thin
1 to 2 cloves garlic, minced
2 to 3 ribs celery, sliced thin
1 14.5-oz can chicken broth
1 15-oz can or 1/4 pound fresh
  bean sprouts, well rinsed
1 8-oz can sliced water
  chestnuts, drained well
1 8-oz can sliced bamboo
  shoots, drained well
soy sauce to taste
salt and black pepper,
  to taste

Moody's Diner Chicken & Rice Casserole

1. Preheat oven to 350 degrees. Grease 9 x 13-inch casserole pan.

2. Combine rice, soups, and water; pour into casserole.

3. Top with chicken breasts, skin side up.

4. Bake 1 hour or until chicken is cooked through and sauce is bubbling.

Serves 4

1 cup long-grain white rice
1 pkg onion soup mix
1 10-oz can cream of
    mushroom soup
2 cups water
4 or 5 chicken breasts

Blue Comet Lounge Crab Cakes

1. Mix together all ingredients except bread crumbs and butter, handling mixture as little as possible. Add just enough bread crumbs to keep mixture together.

2. Form mixture into slightly rounded patties.

3. Melt butter in skillet over medium heat.

4. Sauté cakes 2–3 minutes on each side. Serve piping hot with either cocktail or tartar sauce and a lemon wedge.

Makes about 8 crab cakes

1 pound lump crabmeat
1 tbsp mayonnaise
1 tbsp Worcestershire sauce
1 tbsp parsley, chopped fine
1 tbsp baking powder
1 tsp Old Bay seafood seasoning (or substitute same total amount of celery salt and allspice)
1 egg, beaten
1 tsp crushed garlic
1/4 tsp salt
juice of 1 lemon
seasoned bread crumbs
1 tbsp butter

French-Canadian Meat Pie

1. Put first seven ingredients in large pot and cover with water. Stir to mix. Turn heat to high. When water starts to boil, turn heat to medium. After about 1/2 hour, turn heat to low. Stir often.

2. Simmer 6–7 hours until mixture has the consistency of gelatin. Put pot in refrigerator until fat becomes firm on top. Remove fat with large spoon.

3. Preheat oven to 400 degrees.

4. Reheat meat mixture until it is warmed through and liquefied. Using a slotted spoon, drain mixture and fill pie crust, using a bit of liquid to keep pie moist. Place top crust over mixture; make slits in crust.

5. Bake 15 minutes; then lower heat to 350 degrees and bake about 25 minutes more or until crust turns golden brown. Remove from oven, let cool slightly, and serve warm (with your favorite beef gravy, if you wish). Pie will keep in refrigerator for up to a week and can be made weeks ahead and frozen.

Serves 4

- 1 1/2 pounds ground pork
- 1 1/2 pounds ground hamburger
- 1 medium onion, chopped
- 1 tsp ground cloves
- 1/2 tsp ground cinnamon
- salt and black pepper, to taste
- 1 clove garlic, chopped (optional)
- 9-inch unbaked double crust pie shell

Easy Classic Lasagna

- 12 lasagna noodles
- 1 15-oz tub ricotta cheese
- 1 egg
- salt and black pepper, to taste
- 2 tbsps parsley, diced
- 1 quart spaghetti sauce (meat sauce, if you wish)
- 1 pound block whole-milk mozzarella cheese, grated

1. In large pot boil lightly salted water; add noodles. Cook according to package directions. Do not overcook. Drain in colander, run cold water over to stop cooking process, and lay on wax paper until ready to use.

2. In large bowl mix ricotta, egg, salt and pepper, and parsley.

3. Preheat oven to 350 degrees.

4. In 9 x 12-inch casserole, cover bottom with a few spoonfuls of sauce so noodles won't stick. Lay three noodles lengthwise in dish. Using fork layer about 1/2-inch of ricotta mixture atop noodles. Sprinkle a handful or two of mozzarella over ricotta. Scoop spaghetti sauce over everything to cover. Repeat, building layer upon layer, ending with noodles sprinkled with mozzarella.

5. Cover with foil and bake about 1 hour or until bubbling.

Serves 4

Meatloaf with Blue Cheese Sauce

1 egg
2 tbsps milk
1 pound ground chuck
1 pound ground pork
1/2 cup bread crumbs
1 tbsp parsley, minced
salt and black pepper, to
　　taste
1/2 tsp cayenne
1 small onion, diced
sauce (see recipe right)

1. Preheat oven to 350 degrees. Grease 4 1/2 x 8 1/2-inch loaf pan.

2. In large bowl beat egg and stir in milk. Add meats, bread crumbs, parsley, salt and pepper, cayenne, and onion; mix thoroughly.

3. Bake about 40 minutes. Meatloaf should be firm but not dry.

4. Serve hot, with several spoonfuls of warm sauce over each slice.

Serves 4–6

To make sauce:

Heat all ingredients in pan over low heat, mashing cheese and butter to help them melt. Keep warm.

Sauce:
3 tbsps blue cheese
3 tbsps unsalted butter
2 tsps chives, minced
squeeze of fresh lemon juice

Connie's Pastitsio (Greek Pasta Casserole)

1. Heat oil in large skillet; cook onions until softened. Add garlic and cook 1 minute. Add beef, stirring and crumbling until no trace of pink remains. Stir in oregano, salt and pepper, tomato sauce, and cinnamon stick. Cover and cook at slow simmer about 20 minutes.

2. Cook pasta in slightly salted boiling water until barely tender. Drain, rinse in cold water, and set aside.

3. Uncover meat mixture and continue to cook until most liquid is evaporated or absorbed into meat. Remove from heat and set aside.

4. Preheat oven to 350 degrees. Grease shallow 6-quart baking dish or roasting pan. Arrange half the pasta on bottom and sprinkle with half the grated cheese.

5. Remove cinnamon stick from meat mixture; spoon mixture over pasta. Add remaining pasta and sprinkle with remaining cheese.

6. Spoon sauce over top, lightly smoothing with back of spoon. Sprinkle evenly with cracker crumbs.

7. Bake about 30 minutes or until hot and bubbly. Let cool about 20 minutes before cutting into serving portions.

Serves 12–16

1/4 cup olive oil
1 1/2 cups onion, chopped
3 large garlic cloves, minced
2 pounds lean ground beef
1 tbsp dried oregano
salt and black pepper, to taste, divided
1 8-oz can tomato sauce
1 cinnamon stick
1 16-oz pkg thick hollow pasta (such as bucatini or perciatelli)
1 cup grated Parmesan cheese
sauce (see recipe right)
1 cup Zwieback cracker crumbs

To make sauce:

1. Melt butter in large saucepan; whisk in flour and stir constantly until mixture bubbles. Add milk while stirring—the sauce should be thick and smooth. Remove from heat.

2. In large bowl beat eggs, then whisk in sauce in batches. Season with salt and pepper.

Sauce:
1 cup (2 sticks) butter
1 cup white flour
12 cups milk
5 eggs
2 tsp salt
1/4 tsp white pepper

Sam's Diner

U.S. Route 1 & 301 — 3 miles South of Richmond, Virginia

"AIR-CONDITIONED" — OPEN 24 HOURS

Breakfast — Lunch — Dinner: Steak — Chops — Seafood

Sandwiches & Beverages

"We Serve and Sell SMITHFIELD'S world famous old Virginia ham"

(We ship them the World over)

I ate here!
Guess?

Margaret R Cole
74 Merriman St
Rochester
NY

POST CARD

HIRE THE HANDICAPPED
IT'S GOOD BUSINESS

UNITED STATES POSTAGE

RICHMOND
OCT 13
11 30 AM
2 1952
VA

MELLINGER STUDIOS, LANCASTER, PENNA.

Perfect Roast Chicken

1. Preheat oven to 425 degrees. Wash chicken inside and out (removing gizzards and discarding or using them to make gravy if you wish). Pat dry with paper towels.

2. Set chicken on rack in middle of roasting pan. Drizzle lightly with oil. Sprinkle salt, pepper, and thyme over skin. Insert a meat thermometer in the breast.

3. Roast chicken uncovered 25 minutes on middle rack of oven. Lower heat to 325 degrees and roast 1–1 1/2 hours more, depending on size. Baste occasionally with pan juices. Chicken is done when breast temperature is 170–175 degrees.

4. Let sit 10 minutes, loosely covered with foil, before carving. Serve with Real Mashed Potatoes (see page 51).

Serves 2–4

1 5- to 7-pound roasting
    chicken
salt and black pepper,
    to taste
2 tsp dried thyme
oil

Pork Roast with Mustard Crust

1. Preheat oven to 400 degrees. Wash roast and pat dry. Trim fat, leaving some.

2. In small bowl mix oil, mustard, and thyme. With hands smear roast with mixture.

3. Set roast fat side down on rack in middle of roasting pan. Grind pepper over mixture; it will stick to the mustard coating.

4. Flip over roast and grind more pepper on fat side. Insert meat thermometer. If desired, add 1/2 inch of water in pan so drippings don't burn.

5. Reduce temperature to 325 degrees. Roast, fat side up, 1 1/2–2 hours, checking temperature frequently after the first hour. Doneness is a matter of taste. Pork is safe to eat with an internal temperature of 140 degrees, but that's very pink; 145 degrees is medium-rare, 155 degrees is well-done.

6. Remove from oven; let sit about 10 minutes loosely covered with foil for a juicier roast. Serve with applesauce, roasted potatoes, or both.

Serves 4–6

1 5- to 7-pound boneless pork loin roast
1 tbsp olive oil
1 tbsp Dijon mustard
1 tsp dried thyme
freshly ground black pepper, to taste

Betsy's Shepherd's Pie

1 cup chicken gravy
1/4 cup white wine
3 cups cooked chicken, cut
    into bite-size pieces
1 tbsp white flour
1 tsp Bell's poultry seasoning
    (or substitute same total
    amount of oregano
    and sage)
1/2 cup diced carrots
1/2 cup peas
1 cup pearl onions
salt and black pepper,
    to taste
3 cups mashed potatoes
2 tbsps butter, diced
2 tbsps grated Parmesan
    cheese

1. Preheat oven to 350 degrees; butter large casserole dish.

2. In small saucepan heat gravy, stir in wine, and set aside.

3. In large bowl toss chicken with flour and Bell's seasoning until coated. Transfer to casserole dish; add carrots, peas, and onions; mix lightly. Pour on gravy-wine mixture; stir until everything is well coated. Add salt and pepper.

4. Carefully spread potatoes over top. Distribute butter over surface evenly. Sprinkle with cheese.

5. Bake about 30 minutes or until potatoes are lightly browned and filling is bubbling.

Serves 4

102

Vegetable Frittata

1. Boil potato until cooked but not mushy, about 10–15 minutes. Slice 1/4-inch thick when cooled, and set aside.

2. Preheat oven to 400 degrees.

3. Heat oil in saucepan. Sauté onion in oil a few minutes until soft. Using a spatula, spoon onions and oil into 9-inch pie dish or similar-size casserole.

4. Arrange single layer of potato slices over onions. Add single layer of ham over potatoes, sprinkle on thyme, and add single layer of cheese.

5. Beat eggs in large mixing bowl. Add parsley and stir.

6. Trickle egg-parsley mixture carefully over cheese layer, taking care not to dislodge layers. Sprinkle plenty of pepper on top.

7. Bake about 25 minutes or until surface is golden brown and eggs are set.

Serves 4

1 medium potato, unpeeled
1 tbsp olive oil
1 medium onion, diced small
4 to 6 slices good-quality
    deli ham, diced
1 tsp dried thyme
1 cup grated cheese
    (cheddar, swiss, gruyère,
    or a combination)
10 eggs
1/4 cup fresh parsley, minced
ground black pepper,
    to taste

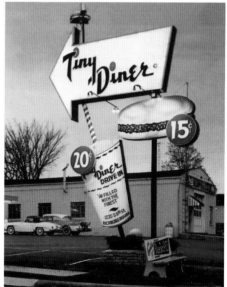

Pub-style Fish 'n' Chips

1. Put oil in large, dry pot around 6 inches deep (but no more than halfway); heat gradually.

2. Mix flour, salt, pepper, butter, egg yolks, and beer in large bowl; beat well. Set batter aside.

3. Wash and dry potatoes thoroughly; cut into uniform strips about 1/2-inch wide.

4. For best results, make sure oil is sufficiently hot before cooking. The perfect temperature is 365 degrees. If you can't check with a thermometer, drop in a 1-inch cube of bread; it should brown in 1 minute.

5. Fry potatoes. Remove with slotted spoon to drain on paper towels; keep warm.

6. Dredge the fish in the batter until well-coated but not dripping; drop into hot oil quickly and decisively. Cook until golden brown.

7. Serve with malt vinegar and plenty of paper towels.

Serves 2

oil
1 cup white flour
1/2 tsp salt
1/2 tsp black pepper
1 tbsp butter, melted
2 egg yolks, beaten
1/2 cup beer
2 or 3 large baking potatoes
1 to 2 pounds fish fillet
   (flounder, haddock, or cod)

Oasis Coffee Shop, U. S. Route No. 1, Holly Hill, Fla.

Salmon Burgers

1. In large bowl break salmon into flakes with fingers or fork. Add cracker crumbs, onion, and celery.

2. In small bowl beat eggs, pour into salmon mixture, and stir to blend. Add salt, pepper, and paprika; stir well.

3. Form 4–6 firmly pressed patties.

4. Melt butter in large saucepan over medium-hot heat. When butter is sizzling but not browning, add patties but don't crowd them. Cook in batches if necessary. Sauté until brown on both sides. Serve with mixed green salad.

Serves 4–6

2 cups cooked salmon
1/2 cup cracker crumbs
  (matzo or Ritz are best)
1/2 cup onion, minced small
1/4 cup celery, minced small
2 eggs
salt and black pepper,
  to taste
pinch paprika
2 tbsps butter

Homemade Mac & Cheese

1. Preheat oven to 350 degrees; butter a 6 x 9-inch casserole dish.

2. Melt butter in large saucepan over medium-low heat; whisk in flour until smooth. Add salt and pepper. Gradually add milk, stirring constantly. Add cheese, stirring until completely melted.

3. Spoon macaroni into casserole and pour cheese sauce over it. Bake 30 minutes or until bubbling.

Serves 4

2 tbsps butter, plus
  additional for buttering
3 tbsps white flour
salt and black pepper,
  to taste
2 cups milk
2 cups grated cheddar
  cheese
2 cups elbow macaroni,
  cooked and drained

Southwestern Stuffed Shells

20 large pasta shells
1 egg
1 15-oz tub ricotta cheese
3/4 cup grated Monterey Jack
  cheese
salt and black pepper, to
  taste
1/3 cup fresh cilantro,
  minced
sauce (see recipe right)

Sauce:
olive oil
1 medium onion, diced
1 28-oz can crushed tomatoes
4 tbsps medium salsa
1/2 cup red wine
1 tsp sugar

1. Boil shells according to directions; drain and set aside to cool.

2. Beat egg in large bowl; mix in cheeses. Add a little salt and pepper; stir in cilantro.

3. Preheat oven to 350 degrees. Spoon sauce into 9 x 12-inch baking dish.

4. Fill each shell with 1–2 teaspoons cheese filling; set into sauce in rows. Baking dish should fill with 20 shells.

5. Bake 15–20 minutes or until cheese has melted and sauce is bubbling. Serve in bowls or deep dishes to enjoy the sauce with the shells.

To make sauce:

1. In large saucepan, heat oil and sauté onion until soft.

2. Pour in tomatoes, add salsa, wine, and sugar; stir well. Simmer 5 minutes.

Serves 4

Chicken Freddie with Mushrooms

1. Heat oil in large skillet. Partially fry chicken. Put flour and paprika in paper bag, shake well, add chicken pieces, and shake to coat. Fry until browned on each side. Blot excess oil with paper towels. Set aside in large casserole.

2. Add onion to skillet and sauté a few minutes until soft. Remove with slotted spoon and distribute over chicken.

3. Leave about 1 tablespoon oil in skillet. Reheat oil; sauté mushrooms just until soft. They will release some moisture. Remove with slotted spoon; sprinkle over chicken and onions.

4. Remove oil and mushroom water from skillet; wipe almost clean, leave a few browned bits. Melt sour cream in skillet.

5. Add broth, stirring constantly and vigorously so it blends with the sour cream. Add tomato paste; stir until well blended.

6. Pour sour cream mixture into casserole. Sprinkle cheese over everything, then almonds. Bake at 350 degrees for about 45 minutes or until chicken is cooked through and sauce is bubbling. Serve over rice.

Serves 4

1/4 to 1/2 cup oil
8 chicken pieces
(preferably breasts)
1 cup white flour
1 tsp paprika
1 large onion, diced
2 cups mushrooms, sliced
1 6-oz container sour cream
1 10-oz can beef broth
1 tbsp tomato paste
1 cup grated cheddar cheese
1/2 cup almonds, sliced

Nick's Diner Lamb Stew

1. Put lamb, onion, dill, allspice, cinnamon stick, bay leaf, salt, and pepper in large pot; barely cover with water. Bring to boil, lower heat, and simmer 1 hour or until meat is tender.

2. Remove meat to a plate. Discard bay leaf and cinnamon stick.

3. Sprinkle flour directly into pot and whisk well to make gravy.

4. Return meat to pot and reheat. Serve with new potatoes.

Serves 4–6

3 pounds lamb shoulder
meat, cubed
1 large onion, diced
4 tbsps fresh dill, chopped
1/2 tsp allspice
1 cinnamon stick
1 bay leaf
salt and black pepper,
to taste
1/4 cup white flour

Make Room for Dessert

How sad it is that people ever have to refuse dessert. Those concerned with health issues forego that final and most satisfying of courses and miss out on so much. In the diner, where the atmosphere presents a feast for nearly all our senses, passing on desserts like homemade apple pie renders the experience incomplete.

Even when we're convinced we cannot possibly eat another bite, we'll rarely say no to great homemade dessert. We visited nearly a dozen diners the day we began a lengthy road trip in Pittsburgh, continued north through the rugged beauty of the Allegheny National Forest and the Finger Lakes Region, and ended at the fabled Highland Park Diner in Rochester, New York. We barely had room for the coffee we ordered merely to justify sitting at the counter in this busy roadside gem. But before we could take our first sips, we caught a glimpse of the apple pie. Even with a quick glance, we knew it was no store-bought pie. The large portions displayed layers of freshly baked filling, gently blanketed with a crust flaky and browned to perfection.

The pie called out to us. Somewhere in our stomachs we'd find room. Hundreds of miles from home, we had no way of knowing when we might return. We had to seize the moment.

We were right. The pie had a slight crunch from the firmness of its apples. The filling, though sweet, did not coat the mouth with a sugary film. It had not

a drop of the sticky goo that too often entangles apples in the assembly-line version. From first bite to last, we drifted through dessert nirvana. Our waitress left us alone to enjoy the intimate moment.

To us pie is elemental, and apple pie provides the true litmus test of dessert

making. We do recognize that some prefer to use bread pudding or rice pudding as benchmarks. Sometimes they are safer bets, especially if you're in large diners. There you may also encounter the famous rotating dessert case displaying some truly monumental cakes. Intended to spark appetites, their architectural qualities probably inspire more awe in construction than in anticipation of culinary greatness. But here, at the Highland Park, the pie case was a diorama, a show within the show of the diner's intimate theater.

And yet, their whimsical qualities add to the overall experience and the growing lore of the great American diner in all its forms. Though we also struggle with our waistlines and take care to control our diets, we will gladly give in to the joys of a fine diner dessert, especially when made by a chef with a passion for the craft. To us, a great dessert in such a place is truly a slice of life itself.

Crumb-topped Apple Pie

1. Mix apples and lemon juice in bowl.

2. Melt butter in large skillet; stir in sugar and cinnamon. Add apples and sauté until slightly crisp, about 5 minutes.

3. Whisk cider and cornstarch in small bowl. Add mixture to skillet and stir. Increase heat and cook until nearly boiling to thicken. Stir constantly so mixture doesn't stick. Remove from heat and let cool completely.

4. Meanwhile, prepare the topping and preheat the oven to 350 degrees.

5. Spoon cooled filling into pie shell; sprinkle topping over filling. Bake until topping is golden brown, 35–40 minutes.

To make topping:

1. Blend all topping ingredients, except butter, with fork.

2. Mix in butter using fingers until moist clumps form.

Serves 6–8

8 to 10 medium apples, peeled, cored, and cut into chunks (Baldwin is best, but Gravenstein, Northern Spy, and Granny Smith are good choices)
1 tbsp lemon juice
2 1/2 tbsps butter
1/4 cup sugar
1 tsp ground cinnamon
2 tbsps apple cider
1 tsp cornstarch
1 9-inch baked single crust pie shell
topping (see recipe right)

Topping:
1/2 cup white flour
1/4 cup oats
1/4 cup white sugar
1/2 cup brown sugar
3/4 walnuts, chopped
1 tsp ground cinnamon
1/4 tsp salt
6 tbsps butter, cut into small pieces

Suzi's Banana Bread

1. Preheat oven to 350 degrees. Lightly oil 9 x 5-inch loaf pan.

2. Mix butter and sugar together in large bowl until very light and creamy. Beat in egg.

3. Mash bananas and buttermilk in another bowl until blended. Stir in butter-sugar-egg mixture.

4. Combine flours, salt, and baking powder in third bowl. Add to buttermilk mixture in two or three batches, stirring after each addition only to mix. Don't overmix.

5. Pour mixture into pan and bake 50–60 minutes or until golden brown on top. Cool 10 minutes in pan; turn out on rack to finish cooling.

Serves 6–8

1/2 cup butter, softened at room temperature
3/4 cup brown sugar
1 egg
2 large bananas
1/4 cup buttermilk
1 cup whole-wheat flour
1/2 cup white flour
1 tsp salt
2 tsp baking powder

CHOOSABANANA!

Jill's Banana Caramel Pie

1. After making the crust, raise heat to 450 degrees.

2. Pour milk into glass loaf pan. Cover with foil and place in larger pan. Fill larger pan with about 1 inch of water. Bake 1 1/2–2 hours, checking frequently near the end. Milk should be golden brown and a bit gloppy.

3. Slice bananas into cooled pie crust.

4. When milk filling is ready and still hot, use a spatula to remove it from the pan and to press it over the bananas.

5. Chill a few hours or overnight.

6. Beat whipping cream in large bowl at medium speed until soft peaks form.

7. Top chilled pie with whipped cream. Crush candy bar and sprinkle bits over whipped cream.

graham-cracker pie crust
  (see recipe below)
1 14-oz can sweetened
  condensed milk
3 ripe bananas
1/2 pint whipped cream
1 Heath candy bar, crushed

To make pie crust:

1. Preheat oven to 350 degrees.

2. Make cracker crumbs in blender and pour into 9-inch pie dish. Stir in sugar and cinnamon. Pour in butter and mix with fork until dry ingredients are well moistened. Press crust into place; bake 5 minutes. Remove from oven.

Serves 4–6

Graham-cracker pie crust:
1 package graham crackers
  (about 9 crackers)
1/4 cup sugar
1 tsp cinnamon
6 tbsps butter

Highland Park Diner Berry Torte

To make berry filling:

1. Place blueberries in one saucepan and raspberries in another.

2. Add 1/4 cup sugar to blueberries and 1/2 cup sugar to raspberries.

3. Simmer 1 hour until very thick. Cool, then chill in refrigerator for a few hours or overnight.

To make frosting:

1. Melt white chocolate in double boiler.

2. Beat butter in large bowl until light, using electric mixer. Gradually add cream cheese until just combined. Beat in vanilla and almond extracts, add powdered sugar, and beat until smooth.

3. Add melted chocolate and beat until just combined.

4. Stir in sour cream. Chill until mixture reaches spreadable consistency.

To make cake:

1. Preheat oven to 325 degrees. Grease three 8-inch round cake pans.

2. Cream butter and sugar.

3. Sift cake flour before measuring. Re-sift twice with salt and baking powder.

4. Add flour mixture to butter-sugar mixture, alternating with milk. Beat until smooth after each addition. Add vanilla and almond extracts.

5. Beat egg whites until stiff but not dry; fold lightly into cake batter.

6. Pour into pans. Bake 40 minutes or until toothpick inserted comes out clean. Cool on wire racks.

To assemble torte:

1. Cut each cake in half horizontally to make six thin layers.

2. Spread the first layer with a thin layer of frosting then half the chilled raspberries.

3. Frost and stack each remaining layer. Leave every other layer without berries; add blueberries to the third layer and raspberries to the fifth layer.

4. Use remaining frosting for sides and top. Chill 1 hour.

Serves 16

Berry filling:
1 10-oz bag frozen
   blueberries
2 10-oz bags frozen
   raspberries
3/4 cup sugar, divided

Frosting:
7 oz. white chocolate,
   chopped
1 1/8 cups (2 sticks plus 2
   tbsps) unsalted butter, at
   room temperature
3 8-oz pkgs cream cheese, at
   room temperature
1 1/2 tbsps vanilla extract
3/4 tsp almond extract
3 1/2 cups powdered sugar
1/2 cup sour cream

Cake:
1 cup butter
2 cups sugar
3 1/2 cups cake flour
1/2 tsp salt
3 1/2 tsps baking powder
1 cup milk
1 tsp vanilla extract
1 tsp almond extract
8 egg whites

Maine Diner Blueberry Pie

7 cups frozen blueberries
1/2 cup plus 1 or 2 tsps sugar, divided
1/4 tsp ground nutmeg
1 tsp fresh lemon zest
pinch salt
1/4 cup plus 1 tbsp cold water
1/4 cup plus 1 1/2 tsps cornstarch
1 tbsp heavy cream
1 9-inch unbaked double crust pie shell

1. In large saucepan combine blueberries, 1/2 cup sugar, nutmeg, lemon zest, and salt. Cook over medium-low heat about 30 minutes. Berries will cook down and become level with liquid.

2. Increase heat and bring to a boil. Stir in water and 1/4 cup cornstarch. Cook 30 seconds.

3. Pour berry filling into large bowl. Cover with plastic wrap; poke vent holes in wrap to prevent skin forming. Place bowl in refrigerator to cool.

4. Preheat oven to 350 degrees.

5. Spoon filling into pie shell. Dust top of filling with remaining 1 1/2 teaspoons cornstarch.

6. Cover filling with top crust and trim edges. Brush top with cream and dust with remaining 1–2 teaspoons sugar. Poke a few vent holes in top crust so steam can escape.

7. Bake 40–45 minutes or until top crust is golden brown.

Serves 6–8

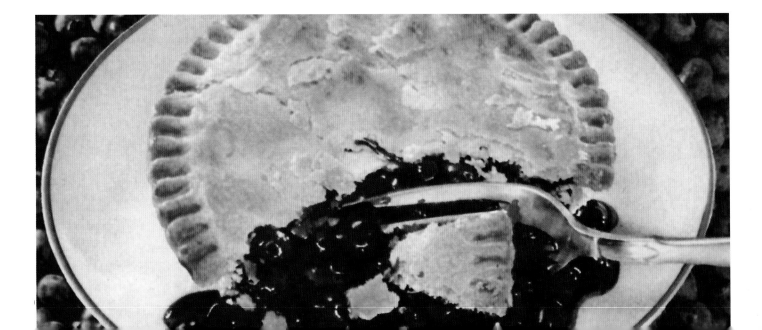

Riverhead Grill Bread Pudding

1. Preheat oven to 350 degrees.

2. Mix eggs, vanilla extract, and almond extract well. Stir in milk. Add 2 1/4 cups sugar, salt, nutmeg, and cinnamon. Add rolls; stir to be sure they are coated.

3. Pour into ungreased hotel-size pan, about 9 x 18 inches; place in shallow pan of water before putting in oven.

4. Bake 1 hour 20 minutes.

5. Cool slightly; mix cinnamon and sugar; sprinkle over top. Serve warm or cold.

Serves 15

12 eggs
3 tbsps vanilla extract
1 tsp almond extract
3 quarts cold milk
2 1/4 cups sugar, plus
    additional for sprinkling
pinch salt
1 tsp ground nutmeg
2 tsps ground cinnamon,
    plus additional
    for sprinkling
5 hard rolls, cut into pieces

Hot Tin Roof Sundae

1. Soften ice cream a bit. Stir in most of the peanut brittle and refreeze.

2. When ready to serve, warm sauce, scoop ice cream into bowls, and pour a scoop of sauce over ice cream.

3. Garnish with bits of peanut brittle.

Serves 2–4

1 pint good-quality vanilla
    ice cream
2/3 cup peanut brittle,
    broken into small bits,
    divided
1/2 cup hot fudge sauce

Canadian Chocolate Cake

2 cups white flour
2 cups sugar
1/2 cup unsweetened cocoa
  powder
1/2 cup butter, at room
  temperature
2 cups hot black coffee
2 eggs
2 tsps baking soda
2 tsps baking powder
1 tsp salt
frosting (see recipe right)

1. Preheat oven to 350 degrees. Grease and flour two 9- or 10-inch cake pans.

2. Blend flour, sugar, and cocoa in large bowl.

3. Blend butter and coffee in another bowl; add to flour mixture and mix until smooth.

4. Beat eggs in another bowl. Add baking soda, baking powder, and salt. Add to flour mixture; mix until smooth.

5. Divide batter equally in pans; bake 35–40 minutes.

6. Frost cake after it has cooled completely.

To make frosting:

1. Mix milk, butter, and flour in saucepan; cook until thick. Let cool.

2. Blend in sugar, shortening, and vanilla extract; beat until silky smooth.

Serves 6–8

Frosting:
1 cup milk
4 tbsps butter
3 tbsps white flour
1/2 cup sugar
1/2 cup shortening
1 tsp vanilla extract

28 FLAVORS

BANANA	COCOANUT	PEACH
BLACK RASPBERRY	COFFEE	PEANUT BRITTLE
BURGUNDY CHERRY	FROZEN PUDDING	PECAN BRITTLE
BUTTER PECAN	FRUIT SALAD	PEPPERMINT STICK
BUTTERCRUNCH	FUDGE RIPPLE	PINEAPPLE
BUTTERSCOTCH	LEMON STICK	PISTACHIO
CARAMEL FUDGE	MACAROON	STRAWBERRY
CHOCOLATE	MAPLE WALNUT	STRAWBERRY RIPPLE
CHOCOLATE CHIP	MOCHA CHIP	VANILLA
	ORANGE PINEAPPLE	

Steel Trolley Diner Oatmeal Pie

- 1 cup white sugar
- 1 3/4 cups brown sugar
- 1 cup walnuts, chopped
- 1 cup coconut
- 1 cup oatmeal
- 5 eggs
- 1 1/4 cups milk
- 1 tsp vanilla extract
- 1 1/2 tbsps butter, melted
- 1 9-inch unbaked single
    crust pie shell

1. Preheat oven to 375 degrees.

2. Mix sugars, walnuts, coconut, and oatmeal thoroughly.

3. Beat eggs in another bowl. Add milk, vanilla extract, and butter. Mix into sugar mixture.

4. Pour mixture into pie shell and bake 45–60 minutes.

Serves 6–8

Martindale Chief Peach-Raspberry Pie

1. Preheat oven to 425 degrees.

2. Mix fruit, sugar, and tapioca in large bowl. Let sit about 15 minutes.

3. Spoon filling into pie shell.

4. Bake 40–45 minutes or until bubbling. Cool before slicing.

Serves 6–8

1 cup fresh raspberries
4 cups fresh peaches, peeled and diced
1 cup sugar
1/4 cup quick-cooking tapioca
1 9-inch unbaked single crust pie shell

Sunny Day Diner's Coconut Custard Pie

1. Preheat oven to 325 degrees. Place cookie sheet in oven.

2. Drain fat from coconut milk. Save 2/3 cup fat and discard the rest. Soften fat in microwave if necessary.

3. Beat together brown sugar and reserved coconut fat in large bowl until fluffy. Add eggs, one at a time. Mix in flour, salt, vanilla extract, coconut milk, and milk. Stir in coconut.

4. Brush inside of pie shell with butter. Add filling. Set pie shell atop cookie sheet in oven; bake 35–40 minutes. When pie is done, top should be puffed up and pie should barely wiggle.

Serves 6–8

1 13.5-oz can coconut milk
1/2 cup light brown sugar
3 eggs
2 tbsps white flour
pinch salt
1/2 tsp vanilla extract
1/2 cup milk
1 cup coconut, toasted
1 9-inch unbaked single
   crust pie shell
1 tbsp melted butter

Gibby's Rice Custard Pudding

1. Preheat oven to 350 degrees. Lightly butter 12 x 18-inch glass roasting pan.

2. Beat eggs well in large bowl. Stir in sugar and vanilla extract. Fold in milk and whisk well.

3. Line bottom of pan with rice; pour egg mixture over rice.

4. Gently set pan in larger pan. Fill larger pan about halfway up the sides with water. Check occasionally during baking; if necessary add more water carefully so water doesn't splash onto custard.

5. Bake 30–45 minutes until custard is set and top is golden brown but not burnt around the edges.

Serves 6–8

6 extra-large eggs
3/4 cups sugar
1 tbsp vanilla extract
4 cups milk
1 cup cooked white rice

Julie's Chocolate Zucchini Cake

1. Preheat oven to 325 degrees. Butter and flour 13 x 9 x 2-inch baking pan.

2. Sift flour, cocoa, baking soda, and salt into medium bowl.

3. Beat sugar, butter, applesauce, and oil in large bowl until well blended. Add eggs one at a time, beating well after each addition. Beat in vanilla extract.

4. Mix in dry ingredients alternately with buttermilk in three batches. Mix in zucchini. Pour batter into prepared pan.

5. Sprinkle chocolate chips, nuts, and coconut over top.

6. Bake about 50 minutes, until toothpick inserted into center comes out clean. Cool completely in pan.

Serves 12

2 1/4 cups sifted white flour
1/2 cup unsweetened cocoa powder
1 tsp baking soda
1 tsp salt
1 3/4 cups sugar
1/4 stick unsalted butter, at room temperature
1 cup applesauce
1/2 cup vegetable oil
2 large eggs
1 tsp vanilla extract
1/2 cup buttermilk
2 cups (about 2 1/2 medium) zucchini, unpeeled and grated
1 6-oz pkg (about 1 cup) semisweet chocolate chips
3/4 cup walnuts, chopped
1/2 cup coconut

Indian Pudding

1. Preheat oven to 350 degrees. Grease a shallow 9 x 13-inch casserole.

2. Heat (but do not boil) milk in large saucepan. Slowly whisk in cornmeal. Switch to wooden spoon and keep stirring, constantly, about 10 minutes or until mixture thickens.

3. Lower heat to simmer, add maple syrup, butter, molasses, cinnamon, ginger, and salt. Stir a few minutes until well blended.

4. Pour into casserole and bake 2 1/2 hours.

5. Serve warm with vanilla ice cream or whipped cream.

Serves 6–8

5 cups milk
2/3 cup cornmeal
1 cup maple syrup
4 tbsps butter
1 tbsp molasses
1/2 tsp ground cinnamon
1/2 tsp ground ginger
1/2 tsp salt
vanilla ice cream or real
   whipped cream (optional)

Index